PAM GEMS

Plays One

PAM GEMS

Plays One

THE INCORRUPTIBLE

GARIBALDI, SI

THE TREAT

Q
QUOTA BOOKS LTD
LONDON

First published in 2021 by Quota Books Ltd. 197 Hammersmith Grove, London W6 0NP

website: www.quotabooks.com – *email*: info@quotabooks.com
Twitter: @Quotabooks

Copyright © Pam Gems

Pam Gems is hereby identified as the Author of the Work in accordance with Section 7 of the Copyright, Designs and Patents Act 1988. The author has asserted her moral rights.

All rights whatsoever in these plays are strictly reserved and application for performance etc. should be made before commencement of rehearsals to Rose Cobbe, United Agents, 12-26 Lexington Street, London W1F 0LE, UK. info@unitedagents.co.uk Tel: +44 (0) 20 3214 0800.
No performance may be given unless a licence has been obtained.

This book is sold subject to the condition that it shall not, by way of trade or otherwise, be lent, resold, hired out, or otherwise circulated without the publisher's prior consent in any form of binding or cover other than that in which it is published and without a similar condition, including this condition, being imposed on the subsequent publisher.

A CIP record for this book is available from the British Library.

ISBN 978-1-9162460-7-2

Typeset in the UK by M Rules
Printed and bound by Biddles
Picture of Maximilian Robespierre courtesy of Getty Images
Cover design: TRISTAN

Available from Amazon, Ingram Spark, Quota Books
and all politically correct bookstores.

Pam Gems was born in 1925 in Mudeford, near Christchurch, in what was then Dorset, on the south coast of England. Her father, a Welsh ex-coalminer, died when she was six years old, leaving her mother to bring up Pam and her two brothers on her own.

For most of her childhood Pam's family lived in poverty, relying on charity from the parish church and the Salvation Army. At eleven, she won a scholarship to grammar school, where she excelled but left at fifteen to go to work.

World War Two broke out and, in 1943, when she turned eighteen, she joined the Women's Royal Naval Service, and worked with British and Canadian bomber squadrons. After the war, she took up a government scheme providing further education, and went to Manchester University, where she studied psychology and met her future husband.

Always stage-struck, Pam Gems wrote her first play when she was eight, and was an enthusiastic participant in school plays. At university, she joined the dramatic society, wrote skits, produced and directed. After university, she got a job in audience research at the BBC, which she loathed – but enjoyed being part of a London bohemian scene that included Ted Hughes, the poet, and Robert Bolt the playwright.

After marrying and having her first two children, she moved to Wandsworth in South London, with her husband Keith, and started writing radio plays. This began an extraordinarily prolific writing career that produced over seventy plays and adaptations, many of them performed internationally.

Pam Gems is Britain's greatest female playwright, with only Agatha Christie having had more West End productions.

ALSO BY THE SAME AUTHOR

Betty's Wonderful Christmas
Go West Young Woman
Dusa, Fish, Stas and Vi
Queen Christina
Piaf
Aunt Mary
Camille
Loving Women
Pasionaria
Deborah's Daughter
Marlene
Stanley
The Snow Palace
King Ludwig of Bavaria
Mrs. Pat
Ethel Merman
Not Joan the Musical

Natalya
The Socialists
At the Window
Franz Into April
The Little Mermaid
After Birthday
Up In Sweden
Next Please
Franz Into April
My Warren
The Amiable Courtship of Miz Venus and Wild Bill
The Synonym
The Whippet
The Russian Princess
The Burning Man
A Builder by Trade
The Nourishing Lie

Mr Watts
In Donegal
Cluster
Down West
The Country House Sale
In The Hothouse
Ladybird, Ladybird
Ebba
Guin for Guinevere
Marine
Who Is Sylvia?
You Should Be Pleased He Likes Me
What Luck
An Ordinary Woman
Cedric and Louise

ADAPTATIONS

The Blue Angel
Sarah B Divine!
My Name is Rosa Luxemburg
Rivers and Forests
Cheri

Uncle Vanya
A Doll's House
The Seagull
Ghosts
Yerma
The Lady from the Sea

The Cherry Orchard
Dance of Death
The Father
Hedda Gabbler
Three Sisters

NOVELS

Mrs Frampton
Bon Voyage, Mrs Frampton

CONTENTS

THE INCORRUPTIBLE   1

GARIBALDI, SI   179

THE TREAT   279

THE INCORRUPTIBLE

Maximillian Robespierre

For Trevor Nunn and Ron Daniels

THE INCORRUPTIBLE – designed by FARRAH, and directed by RON DANIELS – was first performed under the title, *The Danton Affair*, at the Barbican Theatre, London, on 4 July 1986, by the Royal Shakespeare Company.

CAST

Maximilian Robespierre	IAN McDIARMID
Barber	DAVID SUMMER
Eleonore Duplay	JANINE GORE
Messenger	THOMAS KETT
Antoine Saint-Just	HILTON McRAE
Georges-Jacques Danton	BRIAN COX
Louise Danton	EMMA D'INVERNO
General Westermann	CAMPBELL MORRISON
Camille Desmoulins	TOM MANNION
Delacroix	GARRY COOPER
Bourdon	VINCENT EBRAHIM
Philippeaux	JULIAN CURRY
Collot d'Herbois	JOHN BOWLER
Lindet	RICHARD CONWAY
Billaud-Varenne	ADRIAN DUNBAR
Carnot	MURRAY EWAN
Barère	PAUL McCLEARY
Secretary	MICHAEL McNALLY
Vadier	ARNOLD YARROW
Lucille Desmoulins	GERALDINE WRIGHT
Lecointre	PATRICK BAILEY
Courtois	JOHN DALLIMORE
Panis	MICHAEL McNALLY
Legendre	MARTIN MILMAN
Freron	MIKE MURRAY
Tallien	KEITH OSBORN

CAST

Merlin	ANDREW YEATS
Legrand	THOMAS KETT
Chaumette	RUSSELL BOULTER
Le Comte D'Estaing	GRIFFITH JONES
Le Vicomte D'Estaing	SIMON ROBERTS
Fabre d'Eglantine	ROGER LLEWELLYN
Herault de Sèchelles	PAUL SPENCE
Laflotte	DAVID SUMMER
Herman	RICHARD CONWAY
Fouquier-Tinville	OLIVER FORD DAVIES
Sanson	VINCENT EBRAHIM
Citizens	MICHELE COSTA, SUSAN HARPER-BROWNE, PATRICK BAILEY, RUSSELL OULTER, MIKE MURRAY, KEITH OSBORN, DAVID SUMMER
Music Director	BRIAN NEWMAN
Bassoon	PETER WHITTAKER
Singer	NICOLE TIBBELS
Costumes designed by	JUDITH BLAND
Lighting by	MICK HUGHES
Music by	ILONA SEKACZ
Sound by	STEFF LANGLEY
Music Supervisor	TIMOTHY HIGGS
Assistant Director	NICHOLAS MAHON
Stage Manager	JENNIFER SMITH
Deputy Stage Manager	ALISON OWEN
Assistant Stage Manager	DIANA DURAN, ROSY FOWLER

FOREWORD

This is the post-production version of an earlier draft of the play, presented by the Royal Shakespeare Company under a different title, at the Barbican Theatre in August of 1986. THE INCORRUPTIBLE is loosely based on a dramatic manuscript, written in 1929, by Stanislawa Przybyszewska called *The Danton Case*.

As I worked through Przybyszewska's confused, obsessive text, I was captured by her tortured spirit, and her psychotic attachment to Maximillian Robespierre. She believed she was a reincarnation of Robespierre's mistress, Eleonore Duplay, and her writings made it obvious that her obsession with him was necessary for her existence. So long as she was with her beloved Maxime, she would not commit suicide.

My portrayal of Georges-Jacques Danton, who was scorned by Przybyszewska, is different. I felt more sympathy for Danton's pragmatism, and his hedonism, than she did, although, like her, I admired Robespierre's cleverness, virtue, and idealism.

If Robespierre and Danton could have worked together, the French Revolution may have had a different outcome. But four months after he had engineered Danton's execution – to save the Revolution – the incorruptible Robespierre was himself dragged (whimpering, with a broken jaw) to the Widow Guillotine.

After my re-imagining of Stanislawa's work was done, and the show put on, she stubbornly refused to leave me. She was so demanding and distracting I couldn't work. So, to exorcize her spirit, I researched her life, and wrote a play about her called THE SNOW PALACE. When, after a year of intense work, the play was finally finished to her satisfaction, she released me – in a glorious shower of light.

Pam Gems

REVIEW

If you want to know what's wrong with contemporary British drama, hurry to the Barbican for *The Danton Affair*. Go along anyway, because Pam Gems's play exhibits such operatic magnificence as is not to be missed. And in its breadth of mind and generous spirit, it stands as a devastating critique of most other new work.

Today's dramatists often crouch, short of imagination and resources, in a posture of introversion and private despair. But with courage and an implicit, out-of-her-time optimism, Gems confronts questions of immense political complexity. The result, so far as home-grown theatre goes, is the event of the year.

The Danton Affair is Gems's version, not of Buchner, but of the Stanislawa Przybyszewska 'stage chronicle,' which also provided material for Andrzej Wajda's (very different) film. Here are a few days in early 1794, during which a bread shortage and assorted street crises accelerate Danton's disastrous assault on the rule of Robespierre. As the philosophical Philippeaux (Julian Curry) puts it: "People are complaining the smell of blood in the gutters is devaluing their properties."

This is not so much a duel of opposites as the dissection of a love-hate affair. Danton (Brian Cox) is rudely healthy, bullish, corrupt, and licentious to the point of violence. A posturing populist and purveyor of 'glistening lies,' he holds the people in contempt. Robespierre (Ian McDiarmid) is sickly, waspish, visionary, and stiffens at the prospect of physical contact. He is prepared to prosecute the Terror to its most bloodily logical conclusion, but betrays a risibly soft spot for the hapless scribe Desmoulins (Tom Mannion.)

Gems makes it clear that the Revolution urgently needs the attributes of both men (just as the least troubled society requires pleasure and principle) but is forced to choose between them.

Their very extraordinariness brings inevitable problems too. This pair are at best superhuman, at worst deranged. Long after his colleagues have recognised their fate, Danton is still madly proclaiming hope. "I am life!" he roars, in the shadow of the guillotine. "I could eat it!"

And the author looks beyond the Revolution to perennially thorny issues of leadership. Danton may be appalling, but he has a better chance of achieving things than the likes of Philippeaux, who is often clearer-headed, or the lachrymose, romantic Desmoulins.

Robespierre simply understands more than his accomplices, but his understanding leads to the Terror. I wouldn't suggest that France then resembles this or any other country now, but a complex world can only be changed by complex and, I suspect, unpleasant people. It is such realities that Gems encourages us to scrutinise.

Brian Cox conquers the Barbican expanses with a virtuoso evocation of self-interested zeal and bloated charisma. McDiarmid rivetingly deploys ghostly stillness, and his unique rhetorical technique. Nobody can move from a bellow to a squeak as effortlessly, or as chillingly.

These are performances it is a privilege to witness. Grandeur can be unfashionable ...but is essential to the arsenal of a healthy theatre. It's nice to know the Royal Shakespeare Company can still muster it, along with the all too rare combination of pace, clarity and vigour.

Against the besmirched splendour of Farrah's design, Ron Daniels's production rises consistently to the heroic challenges of the script.

Jim Hiley. THE LISTENER 24 July 1986

THE INCORRUPTIBLE

CHARACTERS

MAXIME ROBESPIERRE
BARBER
ELEONORE DUPUY
MESSENGER
SAINT-JUST
GEORGES DANTON
LOUISE DANTON
GENERAL WESTERMANN
CAMILLE DESMOULINS
DELACROIX
BOURDON
PHILIPPEAUX
COLLOT D'HERBOIS
CARNOT
BILLAUD-VARENNE
LINDET
BARERE
ROBESPIERRE'S SECRETARY
VADIER
DANTON'S SECRETARY
WAITER
LUCILLE DESMOULINS
YOUNG OFFICER
SOLDIERS #1
SOLDIER #2
SOLDIER #3
SOLDIER #4
FRERON
LECOINTRE
MERLIN
PANIS
COURTOIS
CONVENTION SECRETARY

LEGENDRE
USHER #1
USHER #2
TALLIEN
CHAUMETTE
HERAULT
LE COMTE D'ESTAING
LE VICOMTE D'ESTAING
LAFLOTTE
FABRE D'EGLANTINE
GUARD
CITIZEN #1
TRIBUNAL USHER
CITIZEN #2
CITIZEN #3
CITIZEN #4
FOUQUIER TINVILLE
HERMANN
JUDGE #1
JUDGE #2
JURY FOREMAN
MAN #1,
MAN #2
MAN #3
MAN #4
WOMAN #1
WOMAN #2
WOMAN #3
WOMAN #4
SANSON
ASSISTANT #1
ASSISTANT #2
BARBER #1
BARBER #2
BARBER #3
BARBER #4
CLERK

THE INCORRUPTIBLE

ACT ONE

ACT ONE – SCENE ONE

ROBESPIERRE's modest lodgings.

The sound of a crowd. Marching soldiers. The heavy wheels of a cart. The sounds die away. A CHILD passes, singing. ROBESPIERRE is sitting, motionless, having his hair dressed. In his mid-thirties, he is thin, pale and looks ill. The BARBER holds up a glass.

>ROBESPIERRE
>
>I can't go out like this.
>
>BARBER
>
>Citizen?
>
>ROBESPIERRE
>
>I look like a dying cauliflower.
>
>BARBER
>
>It's because your face is thinner.
>
>ROBESPIERRE
>
>Well, do something! They won't take me seriously.

The BARBER resumes his work. Pause.

>ROBESPIERRE
>
>I hear there are posters all over Paris.
>
>BARBER
>
>I hadn't noticed.

ROBESPIERRE

What do they say exactly?(*With a keen gaze.*)

BARBER

(Clears his throat.)

That there's no bread. And when there is, it costs a week's wages.

ROBESPIERRE

(Lightly)

And the fault lies with the Convention, in particular, the Committee of Public Safety. Is that what they're saying?

The BARBER doesn't reply.

ROBESPIERRE

What else?

BARBER

That someone is coming.

ROBESPIERRE

(Idly)

Oh really? Who's that?

BARBER

Someone who will save France ... a saviour!

ROBESPIERRE

Ah, so that's what they're saying. (*He turns. His gaze is frightening.*) Do they think it's me?

BARBER

(Scared)

Uh ... oh no, sir ... no, no, no ...

ROBESPIERRE

Who then?

ACT ONE

BARBER

Forgive me, Citizen. You hear so many rumours.

ROBESPIERRE

Who? Who's the saviour?

BARBER

(Stammers, in a whisper.)

Georges ... Danton ... ?

A knock saves the BARBER from further interrogation.

ROBESPIERRE

Come in!

ELEONORE DUPLAY, a young woman in her twenties, enters. She is dark, comely, her manner is grave. She does not smile, but watches Robespierre with hungry concern.

ROBESPIERRE

Ah, Leo! Forgive my not rising ...

ELEONORE

My dear, you're up! And so early!

ROBESPIERRE

The weather – irresistible.

ELEONORE

I daresay the floor swayed a little, though, after five weeks on your back?

ROBESPIERRE

Oh, but that adds to the charm.

The BARBER proffers the looking-glass again. ROBESPIERRE glances at himself ruefully.

ROBESPIERRE

The same time tomorrow, Citizen, if you please.

The BARBER bows and goes.

> ROBESPIERRE
> *(To ELEONORE)*

My lioness...

She slides down his body – kissing him passionately.

> ROBESPIERRE
>
> No, Leo, no...oh my dear... *(Then as, on her knees, she kisses him fervently)* No – No!

ELEONORE rises, a hand to her hair, and imitates him perfectly.

> ELEONORE
>
> "Manifestations of love in broad daylight are both tactless and in very poor taste."

> ROBESPIERRE
> *(Laughs.)*
> Fine principles from a healthy man – from a drowned rat rather less convincing.

> ELEONORE
>
> You're sharpening your claws. That means you're getting better, alas.

> ROBESPIERRE
>
> I see. You prefer me with malaria?

> ELEONORE
>
> At least then I see something of you.

Slight pause.

> ROBESPIERRE
>
> A year of revolutionary work, everything set in motion and back to our own lives. I really believed that. Oh Leo, I'm sorry.

ACT ONE

ELEONORE

Don't be.

ROBESPIERRE

No! You must understand ... there can be nothing – ever. My dear, what use am I to you? I'm nothing but an inflamed brain ...

ELEONORE

Shhh –

ROBESPIERRE

When we do achieve a few spasms of lust, I can't afford the exhaustion. And if I come to you rather than a whore it's because I've not the time nor the energy to walk to a brothel.

ELEONORE

At least I can stop you infecting yourself.

ROBESPIERRE

Don't. *(Embraces her.)* I am so grateful to you.

ELEONORE

(Between light kisses.)

Two weeks ...to make you well ... *(Holding his face between her hands.)*

ROBESPIERRE

(Kisses her cheek.)

Two weeks, oh, and a divine time of year! *(He sighs. Breaking away.)* I'm sorry, my dear. Four days – but those I guarantee!

A knock.

ROBESPIERRE

Come in!

MESSENGER

Dispatch from the Committee of Public Safety, Citizen.

ELEONORE

Tell them you can't possibly ...

ROBESPIERRE

Shhh! *(He reads, intense.)* Very well. *(To the MESSENGER:)* Tell them yes.

The MESSENGER goes. ELEONORE closes her eyes in anguish.

ROBESPIERRE

I must be at the Committee of Public Safety in half an hour. Is there any coffee? Don't worry about bread ...

ELEONORE

I'll find some.

SAINT-JUST enters. He is young, cold-featured, with shoulder-length fair hair. ELEONORE bows as she leaves.

SAINT-JUST

Good morning. You're up. Oh, you look dreadful. Did you receive the message?

ROBESPIERRE

Hullo, Saint-Just. *(Calmly filing his nails.)* Yes. Just now.

SAINT-JUST

If you'd given me a free hand a week ago ...

ROBESPIERRE

... you'd have had every radical in Paris behind bars!

SAINT-JUST

(Sits and rapidly signs papers.)
That fool Hébert and his madmen should have been

ACT ONE

arrested six months ago. As it is, God knows what's going to happen.

ROBESPIERRE

Nothing's going to happen. Once again, our beloved extremists are equating violence with virtue. Once again, we point out the error of their ways.

SAINT-JUST

Half measures? From you?

ROBESPIERRE

You're saying guillotine the lot of them?

SAINT-JUST

Before new factions overwhelm us, yes. You've been in bed for six weeks. These days that's a long time. Why the reluctance?

ROBESPIERRE

To spill blood?

He turns away. Paces. He faces SAINT-JUST abruptly.

ROBESPIERRE

Don't you feel it? The edge? Just there, a few steps away? (*His voice trembles.*) I tell you, Antoine, if we don't keep that dreadful instrument under control . . .

SAINT-JUST

It's necessary!

ROBESPIERRE

Why? We're winning the war. We've stamped out looting. Oh come, Antoine, these people aren't dangerous! They're local heroes – populists. If we destroy all those with a bit of life in them . . .

SAINT-JUST

Remove the seditious troublemakers. That's all I'm saying.

ROBESPIERRE

Because they're noisy? Because we don't agree with what they say? Go on like this, you know what we'll end with? Despair! We have enkindled the human soul. And it burns with a very thin flame. Unless we protect it, the people will lose spirit. They'll be begging for cheap bread and slavery once more. What then, my dear? *(With an oblique smile)* A nation compelled to be free at the barrel of a gun?

SAINT-JUST

But we have a crisis!

ELEONORE enters with a tray. ROBESPIERRE takes it from her courteously.

ROBESPIERRE

Thank you. Real bread – how did you manage?

ELEONORE smiles and goes.

SAINT-JUST

I'm sorry. We've been working all night.

ROBESPIERRE

When do we not? There's no sugar, I'm afraid. No-o . . . No need for human sacrifice.

He sits, drinks his coffee.

SAINT-JUST

Allow me to spell out the facts. Reports of an attempt to overthrow the government are everywhere. Our General Westermann, it seems, is most diligently working against us, and may I remind you there are

ACT ONE

forty thousand guns out there in the hands of the Citizens' Army. Secondly, Desmoulins' Journal is all over Paris. Every page incites rebellion against the Committees, and there are rumours, growing rumours of...

ROBESPIERRE

About the coming of a saviour?

SAINT-JUST

You've heard?

ROBESPIERRE

I had it from the barber. *(Tapping the table irritably.)* Has the bull gone mad?

SAINT-JUST

Your coffee's getting cold.

ROBESPIERRE

You said alliances. What alliances?

SAINT-JUST

Between Danton and the Hébertistes.

ROBESPIERRE

Between the Left and the Right?

SAINT-JUST

Yes! There isn't a Commune that isn't infected. Maxime, reports of an imminent coup d'état are coming in by the hour.

ROBESPIERRE gazes out of the window.

ROBESPIERRE

(After a long pause)

Very well. Very well. Stand down the Citizens' Army and call in all arms.

SAINT-JUST

Not enough. (*ROBESPIERRE turns and gazes at him.*)
You're ill. Out of touch.

ROBESPIERRE looks out the window.

SAINT-JUST watches ROBESPIERRE's hands, twitching behind his back.

ROBESPIERRE

Yes, I see. We must send the Hébertistes to the guillotine. Is that it?

SAINT-JUST

The way to save this country is to send Danton with them.

ROBESPIERRE

No.

SAINT-JUST

Why not?

ROBESPIERRE

(Snarls)

'The Man of the Tenth of August?' However, he presents no threat.

SAINT-JUST

Danton, no …?

ROBESPIERRE

The Journal is a different matter.

SAINT-JUST

Yes. (*He slides a look at ROBESPIERRE.*) Whichever way you look at it, our Camille is for the knife.

ACT ONE

ROBESPIERRE

(Sharp)

No, we'll arrest the publisher. Clip a few wings.

SAINT-JUST

(Gives him a copy of the Journal.)

Read it! He openly ridicules you!

ROBESPIERRE

Camille? *(Laughs)* Impudence! *(But he suddenly shivers violently as he takes the Journal.)*

SAINT-JUST

You're feverish! Stay indoors. I'll manage on my own.

ROBESPIERRE

No. It's time I put in an appearance.

He bends to pick up his hat and gloves, and smiles grimly to himself.

ROBESPIERRE

(Murmurs.)

Four days...but those I guarantee...

He makes a sudden, small, strange shrieking sound. SAINT-JUST starts.

SAINT-JUST

(Alarmed)

You're not delirious, are you?

ROBESPIERRE

No. I am myself.

SAINT-JUST

I hope so.

He follows ROBESPIERRE off.

ELEONORE glides in discreetly to remove the tray.

> *Fade to black.*

ACT ONE – SCENE TWO

DANTON's luxurious apartment. Night.

DANTON, a big, vigorous man, in his mid-thirties, is snoring on a sofa. His own snores wake him.

> DANTON
> Louise? Louise? There's no light!

LOUISE, his teenage wife, enters with a candelabrum. She turns to go, but he grabs her.

> DANTON
> I'm sorry ... I'm sorry if I was rough ...

> LOUISE
> It doesn't matter. Don't! (*She tries to escape him.*)

> DANTON
> (*Gently*)
> I really don't have to apologise. (*He smooths her hair tenderly.*) We know what you think of me, eh? Just you wait. Another three days. Then you'll know what this monster of yours is worth. (*Whispers*) How would you like to be the mistress of France?

> LOUISE
> You're drunk.

She tries to resist, but he traps her and begins to pull at her clothing, groaning and grasping without inhibition.

ACT ONE

LOUISE

Georges, please ...

DANTON

Don't you want me?

LOUISE

Please ...

DANTON

(Undressing her.)

Come on – put out the light if you don't want to look at me.

LOUISE

Don't – please, I'm not feeling well!

DANTON

(Broad smile)

You're pregnant! Are you?

LOUISE

I've told you, I don't know! Don't!

She shrieks.

DANTON

My apologies. *(Bows)* You'd better go to bed.

As she goes, he kisses her hair. She shudders. He grimaces, then turns, alert, at a sound.

DANTON

Who's there?

GENERAL WESTERMANN, a fit-looking man in his early forties, in uniform, enters swiftly, and helps himself to wine.

WESTERMANN

It's all up – finished. (*Of wine*) Ugh, women's piss! Complete debacle. Spies on every corner, arrests by the hour, and the Hébertistes are about to sleep with their heads between their feet. Got anything better?

DANTON hands him the brandy decanter.

WESTERMANN

The rumour is they'll stand down the Citizens' Army and call in every gun in Paris. Oh, and Robespierre's back.

DANTON

(*Thoughtful*)

It may be just as well, General.

WESTERMANN

What?

DANTON

To do nothing.

WESTERMANN

What do you mean?

DANTON

Risky business.

WESTERMANN

We have no choice, you've said so yourself! Robespierre destroys the Citizens' Army...without the army... All right, we've made a few tactical errors. We should have moved sooner, as I said. But it's not too late! Take action now. I can make you whatever you want in a week. Dictator. King... By God, you'd look good, Georges!

ACT ONE

DANTON

(*Morose*)

Especially without a head on my shoulders. Is the Convention still sitting?

WESTERMANN

They're reading so many indictments they'll be there all night.

DANTON

I wonder you're still free. You'd better stick close!

He claps WESTERMANN absently on the shoulder and moves away.

WESTERMANN

They won't touch a friend of yours. You know what we should do now? Ring the alarm bells – dead of night. Open up the prisons. Set the mob on the Convention. By tomorrow evening – Paris at your feet! Believe me, Georges, with the English in the north waiting for us to let them through ...

DANTON

Let in the English? Are you mad?

WESTERMANN

(*Out of face*)

But...only a week ago you were saying the same.

DANTON

That was a week ago.

WESTERMANN

(*Humbly.*)

Look, Danton, I know I'm an utter fool when it comes to politics. You're a genius – a hell of a lot cleverer than me – but we need to move. You need to move. It's not as if your hands are clean.

DANTON

Meaning what, Westermann?

WESTERMANN

You've speculated same as the rest of us. Bought more land than any man in Paris –

DANTON

And why not? What do you want me to do? Live like Robespierre? His dreams of eternal glory are far more dangerous.

WESTERMANN

(Slight pause.)

I saw him just now, in the park.

DANTON

Robespierre? Really? What was he doing?

WESTERMANN

Stepped out for some air I suppose. Looked as though he could do with it.

DANTON

He can go and bugger himself. I carry the centre – and the banks – never forget that. Have you read Desmoulins' latest edition? Read it! *(Laughs)* Thanks to Camille, I have the mind of every man in Paris in my pocket!

CAMILLE rushes in. He pauses on seeing WESTERMANN.

WESTERMANN rises to go, but DANTON waves him down.

DANTON

What's the matter?

CAMILLE

They've arrested Desenne!

ACT ONE

WESTERMANN

The publisher? By God!

CAMILLE

Georges, what am I to do? You insisted on the print. I said it was too dangerous. I don't know what to do!

DANTON
(Squints up at him.)

Crawl off to Robespierre if you're losing your nerve. Tell him I stood over you with a whip. He'd like that.

CAMILLE

Don't insult me, please. That man is an enemy of France. I am with you, you know that. But, for God's sake, I need some advice!

WESTERMANN rises, picks up his hat, and takes a last drink.

WESTERMANN

Well, there we are. No alternative! I'll sound out the Commune at once ...

DANTON

No! Do that and we're dead men. Why the hysteria? A publisher's been arrested. Tomorrow they'll let him go. If not, print up with someone else.

DELACROIX enters quickly.

WESTERMANN

Ah, here's your quartermaster. Hey, Delacroix, how are the investments?

DELACROIX
(Aside, to DANTON)

Danton, I need to talk to you.

DANTON

(Aside)

Shut up. *(Aloud)* What's happening?

DELACROIX

Arrests, everywhere – including Hébert himself. Citizens' Army disbanded. People hiding guns all over Paris. They'll be after us next. We're going to have to be very careful. *(To CAMILLE)* Especially you, my friend.

CAMILLE winces.

DANTON

What's the feeling in the Communes?

DELACROIX

(Wags his hand.)

Our main asset is the bread shortage. There'll be riots within a week. I say we move quickly. Either that or leave at once.

CAMILLE

Leave Paris?

WESTERMANN

He's right, Georges!

DANTON ignores him.

DANTON

(Casual)

I hear Robespierre's back.

DELACROIX

He's there now. Speaking in the Convention. You'd do well to show your face, Danton. We need all the help we can get. By the way, Philippeaux's downstairs. I thought you might like to see him.

ACT ONE

DANTON
(With a laugh.)
That po-faced stick?

DELACROIX
(Smiles)
He's known to be honest. They'll listen to him in the Convention.

DANTON nods.

DELACROIX
Bourdon's bringing him up.

BOURDON and PHILIPPEAUX enter.

DELACROIX turns with a charming smile.

DELACROIX
Ah, Philippeaux!

BOURDON
Gentlemen, may I present my colleague ...

CAMILLE
Philippeaux, welcome!

PHILIPPEAUX
Good evening, Citizens.

CAMILLE
Joining the right group at last, eh?

DELACROIX
(An arm on Philippeaux's shoulder.)
Here is a man who will never be led.

DANTON
In politics, brother, that can be dangerous.

CAMILLE

Join us, Philippeaux. We welcome men of honour!

PHILIPPEAUX

Thank you. Most gratifying. However, I do not as yet know what you stand for, gentlemen.

DANTON

Quite simple. We deplore the unlawful dictatorship of The Committee of Public Safety and the Committee of General Security.

PHILIPPEAUX

In other words, the government.

CAMILLE

Our aim is to put an end to the Terror.

DELACROIX

We want a return to sanity and the rule of law.

He nudges BOURDON.

BOURDON

Oh, absolutely.

PHILIPPEAUX

If these are indeed your aims then I should, most certainly, wish to support you. By arresting Desenne...

CAMILLE

Threatening the freedom of the press.

PHILIPPEAUX

Exactly. The Committees have gone much too far.

CAMILLE

Voila! Our aims are the same.

ACT ONE

                   WESTERMANN

What are your proposals? For action?

                   PHILIPPEAUX

My proposals? Gentlemen, I see no simple answer.

They wait. He is forced to continue.

                   PHILIPPEAUX

We can hardly attack the Committees.

                   DELACROIX

Why not?

                   PHILIPPEAUX

Attack the heart of our revolution? No, no. Morally out of the question, as well as extremely dangerous. No. As I see it, we must reduce the powers of our two great Committees, step by step, to their originally defined and legally agreed functions.

                   WESTERMANN

How?

                   PHILIPPEAUX
                (Shrugs, helpless.)

By persuasion, argument ... reason.

Silence.

                   PHILIPPEAUX

Of course, in the last resort ... Should there be no response ... In the last resort, I suppose we must, reluctantly be prepared to take up arms.

                   BOURDON
                   (Nervous)

You mean, have the Communes attack them?

WESTERMANN

Exactly what I've said to Danton! I vote we move at once!

PHILIPPEAUX

General Westermann...please! I'm sorry, I can't agree! Rouse Paris...yet again...to indiscriminate slaughter? People are complaining. The smell of blood in the gutters is devaluing their properties! No, no, no, no, no. (*He wipes his brow with a coloured handkerchief.*) If we should, regrettably, be forced into action, then every Commune must be properly prepared for the moral necessity, otherwise it's nothing more than another coup d'état.

Silence. Some smiles.

DELACROIX

Surely, with a leader of integrity...

PHILIPPEAUX gives Danton a brief, embarrassed, look.

PHILIPPEAUX

Yes, well...exactly. If the leader can be trusted not to abuse the...ah...the...

DANTON

(*Rises.*)

Philippeaux is right. There will be no coup d'état (*Bows to Philippeaux*) – as you so rightly call it. Set the people on the Tuileries, and they could bring us all down.

WESTERMANN

For God's sake!

DELACROIX

(*Warning, to Danton*)

Georges!

ACT ONE

DANTON

No. Our offensive will be constitutional. We cannot, as our new colleague so shrewdly observes, attack the Committee of Public Safety. *(He pauses, seeming to muse to himself.)* But what of the other great source of oppression, gentlemen, the Committee of General Security – the police?

DELACROIX

You can't do that!

CAMILLE

Bravo. Everyone hates the police!

DELACROIX

You'll lose every Deputy of the Centre!

DANTON

(Waves him away, and takes a stance.)

My friends, this is where we begin. We have the support of the people. The people know that, in us, freedom has its last defenders. Despotism must not, shall not, stifle our voices!

Polite applause.

DANTON

Our cause is justice. Our ammunition ... Courage!

PHILIPPEAUX is impressed.

BOURDON

Attack the Police? Robespierre won't like that.

DANTON

Who? What did you say? I didn't hear you.

BOURDON

Nothing, Citizen, nothing.

                    DANTON

The Convention is in the hands of usurpers! Our
sacred task, Citizens, is to restore our beloved
country to its rightful owners – the people of France!
Only then, dear patriots, can we return – gratefully –
to the quiet shadows of peaceful, private lives. Modest
anonymity among the general happiness our only –
but oh how sweet – reward!

He makes a sign to DELACROIX that the audience is over.

PHILIPPEAUX shakes hands with DANTON fervently.

                    PHILIPPEAUX
I share your views without reservation.

                    DANTON
May we count on your support?

                    PHILIPPEAUX
Indeed, you may.

                    DELACROIX
You'll stand with us? In the Convention?

                    PHILIPPEAUX
I shall be proud to open the debate.

                    DANTON
There speaks a patriot. I am honoured to have gained
such a noble ally.

He sees PHILIPPEAUX out. Embraces CAMILLE, who goes, and
turns to BOURDON.

                    DANTON
Tomorrow, my friend, you will follow Philippeaux's
speech and demand a decree of indictment against
the Police.

ACT ONE

BOURDON

Me? Why me?

DANTON

Flank attack.

BOURDON

Why not you? Surely, you're the one to ...

DELACROIX

You're being very cautious, Georges ...

DANTON claps him on the shoulder, ushering them out.

DANTON

Tactics, my friend, tactics – eh, Westermann?

WESTERMANN laughs. BOURDON, at the door, turns to DELACROIX.

BOURDON

What do you think?

DELACROIX

I think it's dangerous. *(He turns back.)* Georges?

DANTON

What is it?

DELACROIX

We need to talk.

DANTON

I know. I know.

BOURDON and DELACROIX go.

WESTERMANN

So, we don't go for a fight?

DANTON

(Sleepy)

No. Break them on the floor of the Convention.

WESTERMANN looks at him skeptically, and takes up his hat, to leave.

>   DANTON
>   (Over his shoulder)
> Sound out the officers in the Communes. Organize
> those you can trust. They'll be looking for friends now
> the little monkey's disbanded them.

>   WESTERMANN
>   (Softly)
> So, you haven't given up? You're still after it?

Excited, he stands over DANTON.

>   DANTON
> On the contrary, I'm fed up to my balls with the whole
> stinking mess. Still, we may as well keep a few well-
> wishers handy.

>   WESTERMANN
> Just in case?

He hovers, pleased. But DANTON gives him a heavy look and turns away. WESTERMANN pauses, then goes quickly.

> *Light change.*

ACT ONE – SCENE THREE

A crowded Committee Room.

MEN are seated around a large conference table. CARNOT, BILLAUD and LINDET, are on one side of the table. ROBESPIERRE, BARERE, SAINT-JUST, and Robespierre's SECRETARY, are on the other. At its head sits COLLOT, the Chairman. The SECRETARY is taking notes.

ACT ONE

ROBESPIERRE

Danton created a revolutionary centre at the Cordeliere Club across the river. Were we of the Jacobin Club so bold?

CARNOT

He incited the city to a riot that led directly to the slaughter on the Champs de Mars.

ROBESPIERRE

Very well. Who held the country together, after the massive defeat of our armies?

CARNOT

Conspired with the Austrians, you mean.

BILLAUD

The incompetence of the First Committee of Public Safety, under Danton ...

COLLOT

He's an embezzler!

BARERE

Maxime, Danton's offered the crown of France to every princeling in Europe!

COLLOT
(From the Chair)

Robespierre?

ROBESPIERRE

Not one of these allegations would stand up in court.

BILLAUD
(Bangs the table angrily.)
Lawyers' tricks! Is that all you have?

CARNOT

Every one of these charges is an established fact.

COLLOT

Absolutely. *(Brief pause.)* However, Citizens, we are bound to ask ourselves. How is it to be done?

BILLAUD

We can't arrest him outright. He must first be isolated from public opinion.

ROBESPIERRE

(Slight pause. Cold.)

In no circumstances will I agree to the summoning of Georges Danton before the Revolutionary Tribunal.

BILLAUD

(After a pause.)

My god. You're afraid of him.

ROBESPIERRE

(Friendly, mocking smile.)

My dear Billaud! Danton is an individual. We are the revolution. I suggest that, instead of devouring ourselves for the pleasure of our enemies, we compel this noisy buffoon to work for us.

CARNOT

How?

COLLOT

Romantic nonsense!

ROBESPIERRE

Oh yes, much less romantic is to cut off heads. Danton is not a criminal ...

Disagreement.

ACT ONE

ROBESPIERRE

He lacks complexity. His is a primitive nature. When he is threatened, he barks – but it's all air. Citizens, his only source of influence was the Journal. And we've removed it! The man is drowning. To behead him would be barbaric.

BILLAUD

You have a beautiful soul, Citizen.

COLLOT

(Growls)

He'll sell us all out.

LINDET

(Bangs the table for silence.)

To treat the Man of the Tenth of August as a common criminal is to insult the revolution!

SAINT-JUST

(Bangs the table for silence.)

There is proof!

ROBESPIERRE

Proof?

SAINT-JUST

Corroborative evidence from independent witnesses of embezzlement.

SAINT-JUST hands documents to ROBESPIERRE who bends his head to look at them.

BILLAUD

So much for the Man of the Tenth of August!

They wait while ROBESPIERRE reads.

He puts the papers together neatly and unhurriedly, then signals to his SECRETARY to leave.

>BARERE
>
>*(Whispers.)*
>
>What's he doing?

The SECRETARY leaves.

>ROBESPIERRE
>
>Gentlemen. What I am to say is for your ears alone. *(He looks at them keenly.)* I, too, believe Danton to be a criminal. However, despite his undoubted, and proven, crimes against the state, he cannot...he must not... be disposed of.

>BILLAUD
>
>*(Shouts above protests.)*
>
>You are afraid of him!

>ROBESPIERRE
>
>Citizens, we are not here to dispense justice!

A shocked silence.

>ROBESPIERRE
>
>We are here to fight. A revolutionary tribunal is not a court of law – to prosecute and punish the guilty. It is a weapon to destroy enemies. Make the distinction. *(A slight pause. He looks round the table sharply.)* I say to you, Citizens, that Danton's arrest would push the Centre towards counter-revolution.

Murmurs of protest.

>ROBESPIERRE
>
>We need them! All of them! The rich, the powerful, the influential, every predatory animal. Until we can

ACT ONE

extend our system of government across the whole of
Europe, the neutrality of money is of vital importance.
In executing Danton, we unite those forces against us,
and we condemn ourselves to a reign of Terror.

LINDET

Exactly.

ROBESPIERRE

Thank you. To rule by Terror is to admit defeat.
(To BILLAUD.) Yes, I am afraid. Not of Danton,
but of what will be unleashed if we execute him.
So much so that I will embrace any compromise –
even lawlessness – to save France from so evident
and public a failure. If the good of the revolution
demands baseness from us, so be it. The traitor
Danton will avail himself of an exceptional amnesty.
The dispensation of justice is a luxury in which we
cannot – must not – indulge ourselves.

BARERE

(Sits)

But...what's to be done?

CARNOT

We can't go into the spring campaigns with Danton
working against us.

ROBESPIERRE

He must know that his attempts on the Committees
will fail. His surrender is a matter of days.

Slight pause.

BILLAUD

And if he doesn't surrender, Citizen?

Slight pause.

ROBESPIERRE

Then we will execute him. But I say to you, with all the gravity within my command, that this we must prevent. What is the matter?

VADIER enters, pushing past the protesting SECRETARY.

VADIER

Get out of my way, damn you! *(He pauses, getting his breath back.)* They've swung the vote against the Committee of General Security! *(Gasps for breath.)* They're voting a decree of indictment! You must...you must...

But he is overcome. CARNOT helps him to a seat.

COLLOT offers water.

CARNOT

(Looks up grimly to Robespierre.)

So, Danton's ready to concede?

ROBESPIERRE hurtles across the room, followed by SAINT-JUST.

BILLAUD

Where are you going?

ROBESPIERRE

(Calls.)

Where do you think?

SAINT-JUST

You'll get your policemen back!

He and ROBESPIERRE exit.

The other COMMITTEE MEMBERS crowd around VADIER for information. A yock of laughter. VADIER rises.

ACT ONE

VADIER

I don't believe it! Robespierre – defend Danton?

COLLOT

Who knows what goes on behind those green eyes?

BARERE

No, but wait. The fall of Danton will endanger Camille.

VADIER

What are you saying? The Incorruptible would compromise himself for Camille?

CARNOT

Never! That is salacious gossip!

LINDET

I second that.

BILLAUD

But Robespierre's thinking is right. If we cut down Danton, we shall be forced to increase the Terror.

BARERE

(He groans in anguish at the thought.)

No, please, don't!

COLLOT

What's wrong with the Terror? We agreed on the use of it, in the cause of the revolution. How else do we keep control? If we are not prepared to use extreme measures on behalf of the Republic, there are those on the streets who will!

LINDET

Is that what we're here for? To prey on one another?

CARNOT

It's a question of necessity. The only concern of this Committee, now, is survival!

LINDET

At the cost of human slaughter?

BARERE

(Mutters.)

My God. What a horrible responsibility.

They are restless and uneasy.

LINDET

Impeach Danton? No, It's unthinkable.

BARERE

(Sighs)

We seem to be in an age of the unthinkable.

COLLOT returns to his chair, straightens his papers.

COLLOT

Well, Citizens. The next point on the agenda ...
The dispatches from Geneva.

Light change.

ACT ONE - SCENE FOUR

The vestibule of the Convention.

DANTON is facing the door. From within, we can hear BOURDON speaking, but can't make out what he is saying. CAMILLE enters quickly.

DANTON

Well, my boy, so Danton's finished, eh?

ACT ONE

CAMILLE

Georges, please forgive me. I don't know what was the matter with me.

DANTON

Just fright, my dear, just fright! *(Bear hugs Camille)* Enough... Had enough? You realise what we've done? *(He drops Camille, bellowing with laughter.)* Eight days, that's all I need – eight days! You have the choice, my beautiful Paris – do you want him? Or will you have me?

CAMILLE

You're magnificent! You're a Titan!

DANTON

(Laughs.)

Cheap flattery! No, no, go on. I love it!

CAMILLE

I'd die for you.

DANTON

I don't need you dead, I need you writing!

BOURDON and DELACROIX enter from the chamber.

DANTON

Bravo Bourdon!

CAMILLE

Bravissimo! Vivat Bourdon!

CAMILLE and DELACROIX lift BOURDON on their shoulders.

CAMILLE

Oh! Jump! I can't... ouf!

He staggers and the group tumbles, laughing.

DANTON clasps BOURDON by the hand.

>DANTON
>
>My dear colleague! France gives you her thanks! A week from now, the precious blood of our youth will cease to flow. Freedom, friends!

PHILIPPEAUX enters.

>DANTON
>
>*(Turns)*
>
>Ah, Philippeaux! I congratulate you. A wonderful speech! Something wrong?

>PHILIPPEAUX
>
>Gentlemen, the more I see of you, the less I understand! You go too far, too quickly! If you continue to attack the Committees without an alternative structure, the state will collapse!

>CAMILLE
>
>How do you know we're not prepared? That there isn't a man ready and able to lead France?

He wilts under DELACROIX's warning stare.

>PHILIPPEAUX
>
>*(Looks at Danton)*
>
>Have you been using me?

>DANTON
>
>*(Genial)*
>
>Philippeaux!

>PHILIPPEAUX
>
>Goddammit! You've been using me!

>DANTON
>
>Not at all. If you don't like our aims, why push in with us?

ACT ONE

PHILIPPEAUX

Push in with you? But it was you who pursued me!

DANTON'S SECRETARY runs on.

DANTON'S SECRETARY

Danton!

DANTON draws him aside.

DANTON'S SECRETARY

Danton, they're accusing you of high treason!

DANTON

Names. Who? All of them?

DANTON'S SECRETARY

Not Robespierre. Please – I must go back!

DANTON

(Detains him.)

What about Saint-Just?

DANTON'S SECRETARY

Supports the motion. Oh, my God, it's him!

DANTON'S SECRETARY exits.

DANTON

Out of it – all of you.

DELACROIX shepherds the others out. DANTON remains, relaxed, as ROBESPIERRE enters with SAINT-JUST.

ROBESPIERRE

... yesterday they were still in bud. Extraordinary. A very early spring this year ...

DANTON

Greetings, Citizen.

ROBESPIERRE

(Neutral)

Good-day.

DANTON glares at SAINT-JUST, who looks at him coldly and follows ROBESPIERRE into the chamber. The SOUND OF APPLAUSE on Robespierre's appearance. DANTON moves nearer to the door of the chamber, then strolls away, his face heavy with premonition. The chamber door bursts open, to the brief sound of wild applause. BOURDON rushes on.

BOURDON

Georges! They're on their knees to him already! What am I going to do? What am I going to do? I could lose my life!

DANTON

(Growls)

Fight, damn you.

PHILIPPEAUX enters.

BOURDON

(Pushing DANTON)

You get in there! You're the one who wants to be dictator.

PHILIPPEAUX reacts, unnoticed.

BOURDON

(As DANTON grapples with him)

Stop it! I will not sacrifice myself for you!

DANTON

(With a shove)

Then get in there and save your skin!

ACT ONE

BOURDON

Merciful Jesus! I knew it would end like this ...

He tries to make for the exit, but DANTON turns him back into the chamber. Then he sits, unconcerned.

PHILIPPEAUX

(Softly)

You villain.

DANTON

(Turning casually)

What's the matter, Philippeaux? Losing your nerve?

PHILIPPEAUX

My God, what a fool I've been.

DANTON

Getting ready to inform, are you? *(Turns to regard Philippeaux.)* They'll have your head as well.

PHILIPPEAUX pauses, then spits in DANTON's face, and goes.

DANTON lies back, seemingly sleepy. DELACROIX enters.

DANTON

(Dry)

Running down your legs, is it?

DELACROIX

How many times have I told you? Hang on to the Centre! *(Slight pause.)* You've sent Bourdon to his death, you know that? *(Closes on Danton)* We must leave now. Cross the Channel tonight. Danton?

DANTON

Can I take my country with me on the soles of my shoes?

DELACROIX

Oh, for Christ's sake!

DANTON

Anyway, I've broken with the English.

DELACROIX

You mean they've broken with you. Very well, I've no intention of being slaughtered. I shall now fall ill for two days. You have two days to get me out of this. Or else.

DANTON

You coward! You think I'd be sitting here if...

DELACROIX

Two days.

DELACROIX goes quickly.

DANTON

(Bellows after him.)

Hey...you...Lacroix! Bought any more cargoes lately? How much is Flemish lace these days?

ROBESPIERRE

(Offstage)

Citizens, I ask you once again – what is freedom without law...without order? Do you want a freedom where only the ferocious rule?

CAMILLE backs in, listening to Robespierre.

ROBESPIERRE

(Offstage)

And will you now...mindlessly...give way to a genuinely dangerous faction? This decree has been forced through by specious argument...

ACT ONE

DANTON

Quite right.

ROBESPIERRE

(Off)

I say strike out this decree!

CAMILLE

I'm with you, Georges.

DANTON

Till Robespierre lifts his little finger.

CAMILLE

No! I'm prepared to die for you!

DANTON

They won't turn on me. The people of France would rise up against them

CAMILLE

Bravo! Go in there. Challenge him!

DANTON

No. (He rises) I shall see him privately – acquaint him with his mistakes. No, we must put an end to this bloody farce together.

CAMILLE

You're prepared to compromise, with Robespierre? I'd rather die.

DANTON

You'll get over it. (He listens to applause within.)
That, I surmise, is the end of our decree.

He grimaces and they leave, with CAMILLE glaring back defiantly at BILLAUD and VADIER as they enter.

> VADIER
>
> Time to stuff that fat turbot I think. (*Laughs*)
>
> BILLAUD
>
> The thought of sentencing a fellow revolutionary to death amuses you?
>
> VADIER
>
> You feel sorry for Danton?
>
> BILLAUD
>
> I feel sorry for a country governed by those who think killing is a joke.
>
> VADIER
>
> You sanctimonious son of a whore!

He throws himself on BILLAUD. ROBESPIERRE enters with SAINT-JUST.

> BILLAUD
>
> (*Breaks away from Vadier. To Robespierre:*)
> Perhaps now you recognise the need for action?
>
> ROBESPIERRE
>
> I recognise the need for negotiation.
>
> SAINT-JUST
>
> No ...
>
> ROBESPIERRE
>
> When I have made Danton fully aware of his situation – and I have reason to believe I shall succeed – I will report back to you.
>
> VADIER
>
> Meet with that traitor?

ACT ONE

BILLAUD

You mean to beg Danton for an audience?

SAINT-JUST AND VADIER

No!!

ROBESPIERRE

My dears, what are personal humiliations when the fate of the Republic is at stake? *(He smiles gaily)* I doubt the need to fall at his feet, but...should France demand it...

He gives them a charming smile, bows lightly, and goes.

> Light change.

ACT ONE – SCENE FIVE

A private room at the CAFÉ DE FOIX.

A table set for two. Offstage, someone is singing a love song.

DELACROIX enters with a candelabrum, waving away a WAITER.

DANTON enters, walks up and down. CAMILLE enters.

CAMILLE

Why here? Why the Café de Foix? You should have received him at home in your dressing gown. After all, you're doing the favour.

DANTON

(To DELACROIX)

Is everything arranged?

DELACROIX

The landlord will warn us when he arrives...I'm in there...

He opens a door in the wallpaper.

>DANTON
>Good. Get out, the pair of you. Camille, go home.

>CAMILLE
>And miss all the fun?

They leave. DANTON, alone, shows restlessness. He inspects the table sombrely, and lifts a hand. A WAITER comes on. DANTON whispers to him, then stands over him as he rearranges the covers.

The WAITER goes. DANTON now fidgets with the chair, then his fine waistcoat. He takes a quick glass of wine and moves apart – the better to hear the singing.

ROBESPIERRE enters, sees DANTON at a distance, and clears his throat. DANTON doesn't hear him.

ROBESPIERRE pauses, uncertain, then makes his way to a seat at the table. The SONG ends. DANTON claps, roars a genial 'Bravo,' and turns. He jumps at the sight of ROBESPIERRE – seated, powdered and elegant, and exuding a small social smile. Caught on the wrong foot, DANTON scowls fleetingly, then sits with an expansive gesture.

>DANTON
>*(Too late)*
>Sit down. I've found you some river trout. I thought a
>blanquette de veau to follow, seeing as ...

ROBESPIERRE shakes his head, lifting his hand with a small smile.

>DANTON
>I can fetch some oysters – that suit?

>ROBESPIERRE
>Nothing for me.

ACT ONE

DANTON

Oh. On a diet, are you? You're not frightened of being poisoned? You don't mind if I help myself – I told them to leave us alone.

ROBESPIERRE watches as DANTON heaps his plate and begins to eat vigorously. He looks up from the plate, speaking with his mouth full – suspicious.

DANTON

What did you want to see me about?

ROBESPIERRE

Your machinations are paralyzing the government. However, for certain reasons we prefer to keep you rather than have you removed. If you will agree to give up your counter-revolutionary opposition, and to teach your young parrot, Camille Desmoulins, a few new tunes, we are prepared to guarantee your safety.

DANTON

(Confused by all this)

Why do you come to me with threats? You're forgetting yourself, Robespierre. My only law is the good of the people.

ROBESPIERRE

(Dully)

No speeches. You see, I know you.

DANTON

(Explodes)

And what is that supposed to mean?!

ROBESPIERRE

(Looks at his hands)

It means that I have seen through you. A little late

perhaps. Last autumn, to be exact. I know where
you got your money. I know where, when, and how
you have treated with the enemies of France. I know
of your attempts to save the life of the King, and I
know of your efforts to save the Queen. I know your
attitude to the war – and I know your feelings about
dictatorship.

DANTON

Maxime! Who's been filling your mind with ...

ROBESPIERRE

So, you will understand if I find your references to
the good of the people somewhat lacking in taste.
Until now, I have kept these sad and disturbing facts
to myself. And I am ready to go on deceiving the
public. *(DANTON makes to protest.)* I am ready to
allow you to go unpunished. If ... that is ... I have
your word. *(DANTON listens.)* That you will support
the government. Unequivocally.

DANTON

All right, Robespierre. All right. You have the
advantage. But I tell you – don't ask me to eat dirt!
I won't bend the knee.

ROBESPIERRE

You feel yourself superior to the government?

DANTON

As every outstanding man is to the mob. *(He squints
at ROBESPIERRE.)* Accuse me? Where's your proof?

He pours himself a drink. Drinks deep. Then refills his glass, and
a glass for ROBESPIERRE.

ACT ONE

>DANTON
>
> All right. Let's have it out. Here – since you're not afraid of poison. Your health! *(He drinks deeply again.)* I shit on your government, Maxime. I despise it. As you do. The ring of our contempt encircles the Convention. No, don't deny it! We despise the lot of them. *(He claps ROBESPIERRE heartily on the back.)* With one mutual exception, eh?

ROBESPIERRE, mystified, responds with a neutral glance.

>DANTON
>
> I shall never say this publicly, nor will it ever be admitted to my so-called friends and colleagues. Which is why this particular confession...my first real confession ever... gives me such profound delight. Maxime. I worship you. I adore you.

ROBESPIERRE is openly amazed. DANTON drinks heavily.

His manner now varying between honesty and subterfuge. An uneasy mix.

>DANTON
>
> You know why. Of course, you do. You're greater than I am. You're a man of genius. I've been watching you turn this government into an obedient instrument for your purpose.

>ROBESPIERRE
>*(As DANTON looms, smiling fondly.)*
> What is it you want?

DANTON bows before him like a submissive animal.

>DANTON
>
> I am prepared.

ROBESPIERRE
You mean you concede?

DANTON
I am prepared – to bend the leg, to the only man in the world greater than myself! We'll make a pact, you and I, here and now.

ROBESPIERRE
(Slight pause).
Very well. I've already stated my terms. *(He leans across the table.)* Open and genuine and unequivocal support for the government ...

DANTON bangs the table – affecting Robespierre, who begins to look fragile.

DANTON
Absolutely! With all my heart! From this moment, you have the mind and soul of Danton!

He leans over Robespierre, his face sweating and full of love. ROBESPIERRE, rigid, refrains from flinching away.

DANTON
Mind you ... mind you – you're asking us to sign our death warrants.

ROBESPIERRE
(Immediately suspicious)

What?

DANTON
Maxime! All right, I grant you – magnificent! Political planning worthy of the archangels –suitable for the lush gardens of Paradise. For this earth? For human beings? Lunatic, idealistic nonsense. *(He pushes his face, now ugly, into ROBESPIERRE'S.)*

ACT ONE

Abolish greed...corruption? You may as well try and stop us pissing. Maxime – people work for themselves. What else are they prepared to strive for?

                    ROBESPIERRE

The larger cause!

                    DANTON

They won't do it for you.

                    ROBESPIERRE

Not for me. For virtue.

                    DANTON

And where in hell is the profit in that, now we've abolished God and the hereafter? *(Bellows with laughter.)* Why do you think the masses are with us? We promise a better share-out! *(Refills his glass, waves the decanter at ROBESPIERRE, who shakes his head.)* Pull back, Maxime.

                    ROBESPIERRE
                    (Quietly)

How?

                    DANTON

Abandon Terror.

Unobserved, ROBESPIERRE gives DANTON a responsive glance – then looks away.

                    ROBESPIERRE

Without vigour we decay.

                    DANTON

The inflexible Robespierre. Do you think you can build on mud? People are clay – dirt! Oh, but you're going to make them in your image – a hundred million

Robespierres, all sober and industrious. The new
journeyman society going about its business, gainfully
and obediently employed ... until they turn on you.
Which they will. Make no mistake about that. A mob
can be used ... but as a base? A foundation? No! People
live in imagination, dreams! You have to bring them
to heel not with the whip but with splendour. Love ...
Games ... iced puddings! Sermonizing? Never!

He helps himself to more wine. Waves the decanter to Robespierre, who shakes his head.

>ROBESPIERRE
>(*Stiff*)
>You find the fundamental principles of democracy absurd ...?

>DANTON
>On your terms, yes. You think you can inspire ... and alter ... the people? That noisy mob out there? How many care, let alone understand, the running of their own district? How many know where the water comes from? How steel is forged? Where the money goes on public services? Do they care? (*He leans forward.*) What do they care about? Their own lives!

He thumps the table, making the glasses rattle, to ROBESPIERRE's discomfort.

>DANTON
>How many men in a thousand? One? Two at most. The rest will agree with whatever you say if you shout loud enough. Give most people real freedom and they'll suffocate like fish on a beach. (*Pause.*) Well, Robespierre ... now you know me.

ACT ONE

ROBESPIERRE
(Thoughtful)

Yes.

DANTON

It is true. I did dream of absolute power. What else is there to tempt a man of ability on this miserable earth? But who wants to rule over cattle? Where's the joy in it? I feel nothing but a deadly loneliness, and I think you know what that is. I've watched you sitting there, your body turning to pus. But we're different. You seem to be able to stifle the man within you. My nerves can't manage it. I find I cry a lot, I don't know why. Tiredness I daresay. I've been looking for one man – anyone – anywhere – a woman even. One countenance, one live face among the dead, enamelled mirrors reflecting my own fears, greeds ... No one. Until, one morning in the Convention I caught sight of those hostile green eyes, flashing a live thought across the room. Ecstasy. I saw it, behind that mask of yours. The contempt. And the will – oh yes, the will! ... I curse you for it. Your damned, fatal virtue will be the death of us! But there it is. You're the one. In the whole sour, self-seeking mess. So, I shan't let you go. How can I, now you know my secret? I shall have to bind you close, force you to take the right road. Come, look at me, Incorruptible. Admit it. You feel the same. We're two of a kind. Why disguise it? There's no need to anymore.

A long silence.

ROBESPIERRE

You make me sick.

Silence.

DANTON

You slithering viper. I'm offering you the truth – myself! Very well. Take my life! I've little enough use for it. You want to throw it away? Go ahead. Destroy me. Snatch the crown. See how long it takes to burn your brains into a casserole. Dictatorship? Is that what you want? You of all people? Yes, of course. But you won't do it without us.

ROBESPIERRE

Us?

DANTON

Those of us with the capacity and intelligence to make you whatever you wish – the élite! Put us to work Maxime! You want revolution? To whom will you delegate? Illiterate peasants? Let me bring you witty and practical compromise, the mending thread of good administration. Let those who can achieve it for you!

ROBESPIERRE

I am not interested in serving your élite at the expense of the majority. What matters is ...

DANTON

My dear, our aims are not in doubt. I'm talking about means. Survival. *(Comes close.)* I am prepared to throw the weight of my faction at your feet. Just say yes. One word and, together, we can change the face of the earth. One word. Go on – say it!

ROBESPIERRE rises, and sways in tension and indecision.

DANTON

If you want to be king – very well. It's all the same to ...

ACT ONE

ROBESPIERRE

Excuse me. This meeting has been a mistake.

DANTON leaps on him, shaking him like a doll.

DANTON

You squitting, double-faced runt!

ROBESPIERRE, very frightened, manages to escape. He recovers, and straightens his clothes. DANTON, wounded to the core, becomes calm with hate.

DANTON

You may be interested to know that there are at least four witnesses to what you have just confessed.

ROBSEPIERRE

I assumed so. Which is why I have disappointed them.

DANTON

Maxime!!

He rushes after ROBESPIERRE who turns, looks at him coldly, and goes. DANTON staggers. His jaw trembles. DELACROIX enters, with a deadly smile. DANTON controls himself.

DANTON

You heard, I presume?

DELACROIX nods briefly.

DANTON

A cautious beast, eh? At least now he has some respect for me. I have him in the palm of my hand.

DELACROIX

There is still time. If we go – tonight – we could be in Spain in a week.

DANTON

What are you talking about? You fool, they won't touch me, didn't you hear? They daren't.

He sits, helps himself liberally to food. Gestures to DELACROIX to join him. Delacroix shakes his head.

DANTON

Westermann's been round the Communes. He's certain we can count on at least two thirds of the People's Army. You'd better see him, find out about equipment, weapons.

DELACROIX

When do you need to know – now?

DANTON

No, no, tomorrow ... The end of the week ... On second thoughts, I shall be busy. Make it tonight.

DELACROIX

(Who isn't fooled)

Tonight, eh? *(He whistles.)* Where shall I see you? At home?

DANTON

Yes, yes, yes. I'll take a walk through the Communes. Show my face. It doesn't do to lose touch. Where's Camille?

DELACROIX

Disappeared.

DANTON grimaces in contempt.

DELACROIX

In two hours then? Danton?

But DANTON saunters off with a vague wave of the hand.

ACT ONE

DELACROIX stands, his face set, then makes off quickly in the other direction.

Light change.

ACT ONE – SCENE SIX

Outside the Café de Foix.

SAINT-JUST is loitering. ROBESPIERRE enters.

SAINT-JUST

Maxime ...

ROBESPIERRE starts with a fright. SAINT-JUST, seeing Robespierre feels ill, assists him to a street bench.

SAINT-JUST

Sit down.

ROBESPIERRE sits, waving away his assistance. SAINT-JUST sits down beside him.

SAINT-JUST

What amazes me is that you ever took him seriously.

ROBESPIERRE

We have all misunderstood. He has a remarkable mind ... impeccably logical, dazzlingly imaginative ... such a mind Satan himself must possess. I have been guilty of a fundamental error of judgment. Georges Danton is a source of evil, disease and destruction.

SAINT-JUST

Somewhat intemperate, your use of words.

ROBESPIERRE

Words, yes! What shook France off her foundations in 1789 if not the intemperate use of words?

SAINT-JUST

Words change nothing.

ROBESPIERRE

My boy, sometimes the idiocy of youth in you makes me tremble. Revolutionary actions ungoverned by ideas are worthless.

SAINT-JUST

Precisely. Which is why Danton's influence is no threat.

ROBESPIERRE

On the contrary, those sentimental ravings are pervading every mind in Paris. Oh, they won't fool a man with a trained mind. But how many out there have that advantage?

SAINT-JUST

The answer is simple. Cut him down and his rhetoric disappears like smoke.

ROBESPIERRE

Yes. Danton is a criminal. Infantile. Malevolent...and wholly successful. No wonder Camille was seduced by him. And I thought it was the other way round! There is no alternative. He must be executed at once.
(He rises.) We'll call a plenary session for tomorrow afternoon.

SAINT-JUST

I'll walk you home.

ROBESPIERRE

No.

ACT ONE

SAINT-JUST

Where are you going?

ROBESPIERRE

(Formal)

Good-night.

SAINT-JUST

Why tomorrow afternoon? Why not the morning? Why not tonight?

ROBESPIERRE

(Turns, bows lightly.)

Because such is my pleasure.

END OF ACT ONE

ACT TWO

ACT TWO - SCENE ONE

The Drawing Room in the house of Camille and Lucille Desmoulins.

LUCILLE DESMOULINS, an elegant woman in her early thirties, is pacing. CAMILLE enters. He throws down his coat and kisses LUCILLE.

                        CAMILLE
Is the boy asleep?

                        LUCILLE
Yes, at last. Well?

                        CAMILLE
I heard every word!

                        LUCILLE
And? What happened, tell me!

                        CAMILLE
I'm not sure. Georges laid on the flattery ...

                        LUCILLE
Good! So, there was a reconciliation?

                        CAMILLE
No, oh no. Robespierre lost his temper. *(She shows alarm.)* He's missed his chance. He was offered the hand of friendship. If he refuses, so much the worse for him. Georges is ready to move. He must, to save ...

                        LUCILLE
                    (Embracing him sadly)
Oh, my poor Camille!

ACT TWO

CAMILLE

What are you talking about? We haven't lost.
Why do you do this? You're going to make me hate
you!

The BELL rings. They spring apart in fright, gazing at each other.

CAMILLE

(In a whisper)

Who is it?

She shakes her head.

CAMILLE

(Picking up his coat.)

I'm not at home!

He leaves swiftly. ROBESPIERRE enters.

ROBESPIERRE

Madame.

He bows. Looks up, and sees Lucille is shocked by his appearance.

ROBESPIERRE

I've changed. I daresay I look older.

LUCILLE

(Stammers)

No, no – no, not at all. *(She takes his coat)* It's simply
that Citizen Robespierre is now so important... I
wonder... is there still Maxime, our friend?

ROBESPIERRE

Oh yes. As yet.

LUCILLE

Do sit down. Camille will be here directly. *(Then, low
and quick, at his side)* Tell me, Maxime, are things
going to get harder?

He nods.

> LUCILLE
>
> Please, you must help him! He doesn't think ... He has the deepest regard for you ... Won't you?

> ROBESPIERRE
>
> That is why I'm here.

> LUCILLE
>
> Thank God.

She covers his hand with kisses.

> ROBESPIERRE
>
> But I must have your cooperation.

> LUCILLE
>
> I will do anything. Anything!

> ROBESPIERRE
>
> Then I must ask you to break his association with Danton.

> LUCILLE
>
> *(After a moment.)*
>
> But I couldn't – how? Even if it were possible – no, if I were even to try to intervene, I should risk losing him myself.

> ROBESPIERRE
>
> Might it not be better to sacrifice your own happiness, rather than his life? *(Low and urgent.)* Lucille, for once in your life abandon that exquisite tact of yours and persuade him ...

CAMILLE enters.

ACT TWO

CAMILLE

I said quite distinctly I was not at home.

LUCILLE

Camille! *(To Robespierre:)* I'll see you before you go, Maxime?

He bows as she goes, then sits again.

ROBESPIERRE

Do sit down. It's uncomfortable having to look up at you.

CAMILLE sits ungraciously.

ROBESPIERRE

You are in danger. From tomorrow, the Convention will make no further concessions to Danton and his associates.

CAMILLE

So, you come to threaten me in my own house. I admire your audacity.

ROBESPIERRE

If you are fool enough to believe that Danton's friendship is without interest...

CAMILLE

Any friendship between Georges Danton and me is no concern of yours.

ROBESPIERRE

(Mutters)

I have come here, not without risk, to warn you.

CAMILLE

I'm not afraid of death!

ROBESPIERRE

Of course not, a mere trifle! Camille, you know me well enough. I respect honest friendship between colleagues. But with Danton?

CAMILLE

You have never understood our friendship – nor me.

ROBESPIERRE

Perhaps not. But you do know that I'm honest?

CAMILLE looks up.

ROBESPIERRE

And you know that I make fewer mistakes than most. Camille, you do know that, don't you? So that when you accuse me in The Journal of making errors, you're acting against your better judgment.

CAMILLE gives him a frightened look.

ROBESPIERRE

Oh, I know how convincing Danton can be – how heroic. I've been inspired myself! One wants to believe! *(Suddenly harsh)* You thought that by calling for tolerance, you were saving France. In fact, you are protecting the Royalist cause, which is Danton's intention!

CAMILLE

If he chooses to betray that is his affair. My loyalty is to Danton.

ROBESPIERRE

Very noble.

CAMILLE

Do you want me to hit you?

ACT TWO

ROBESIERRE

Oh, at last – a genuine response! Camille, are you really not aware of the criminal nature of the illusions you've been spreading? There are causes worth dying for ... but for these pie-in-the-sky phrases – which aren't even your own?

CAMILLE

You're a great man, Maxime, but you've always lacked sensitivity.

ROBESPIERRE
(Cheerful.)
I apologise. *(Pause.)* Consider this. You know me to be honest. Is he?

CAMILLE

Oh, go away! You have destroyed everything inside me, you can now rejoice –

ROBESPIERRE

I do rejoice.

CAMILLE

Go away!

ROBESPIERRE

Very well. But I must first have certain assurances.

CAMILLE

God, you must despise me! *(He looks, sees Robespierre smiling cheerfully.)* At least I appear to afford you some amusement.

ROBESPIERRE

You don't change.

CAMILLE
At least I'm capable of suffering.

ROBESPIERRE
Oh please!

CAMILLE
Aha, don't tell me I embarrass you, or does Robespierre never admit to feelings?

ROBESPIERRE
(Soberly)
I admit to the need for friends.

CAMILLE
I'll be anything you want! *(Striking a pose)*

ROBESPIERRE
I want you to free yourself from Danton and his faction – publicly.

CAMILLE
(Grimaces, then ...)
I'll write to him now.

ROBESPIERRE
Tomorrow you will make a speech in the Convention, and in the next issue of The Journal you will retract your previous slanders. That is all.

A silence, then CAMILLE whistles – thrusts out his legs – and bursts out laughing.

CAMILLE
Oh Maxime! Maxime! *(Rolls with laughter)* The same as when we were at school ... the same!

ROBESPIERRE
What is it now?

ACT TWO

CAMILLE

Well! *(Jerks away in fury.)* Now we understand!

He walks about arrogantly, swinging his watch chain.

CAMILLE

It seems the fool has some value! The Incorruptible One, willing to sacrifice his dignity and knock on my door. I wonder why?

ROBESPIERRE, fearing to have betrayed a fondness, shows distress. CAMILLE misreads him.

CAMILLE

Because he's afraid! That's why you crawled after Danton. He kicked you out so you thought – Camille! I can gull that young fool. Well, the printed words of this young fool are lighting fires from here to Marseille! I understand! You're in danger! And who could resist those eyes? Yes, they are beautiful. But I won't commit treason for them.

ROBESPIERRE

You think those are my motives? (*He trembles with fatigue*) Don't you understand? Don't you know me?

CAMILLE

No, I don't know you. I never knew you! I don't understand your damn politics. I thought you were both giants! But it's all lies…all of it.

ROBESPIERRE

Please. If you don't do as I say, you will die.

CAMILLE turns, and sees that it is the truth.

ROBESPIERRE

It may even now be too late.

CAMILLE

(Stunned)

I see. *(He wavers, then mutters)* You'd better go then. Thank you for coming.

He turns and walks out. ROBESPIERRE swiftly crosses, and picks up his coat. LUCILLE enters quickly.

LUCILLE

Oh, but you can't leave. No, please don't go!

ROBESPIERRE

I'm sorry. *(He picks up his cane.)*

LUCILLE

But you came here to help him!

ROBESPIERRE

I'm sorry. I gave no guarantee of success.

LUCILLE

No, don't. You can't abandon him. It's inhuman!

He turns on her. She is frightened.

LUCILLE

Please, don't be angry ... Maxime, I didn't mean ... You can't desert him. *(She holds on to him.)* You're not angry?

ROBESPIERRE

There is nothing to be angry about.

LUCILLE

Oh!! *(Relieved, she smiles.)* Then you'll ...

ROBESPIERRE

I'm afraid it makes no difference now.

He looks at her with sombre intensity, then goes.

ACT TWO

She feels faint, holds the chair for support.

> *Blackout.*

ACT TWO – SCENE TWO

The Committee of Public Safety.

BILLAUD, COLLOT, LINDET and CARNOT enter severally. LINDET takes the chair.

> COLLOT
>
> Why now, in the middle of the night? Surely it could have waited?

> LINDET
>
> There must be a reason.

> CARNOT
>
> I was in bed!

> COLLOT
>
> Asleep?

> CARNOT
> *(Laughs)*
>
> Not exactly. We need to table a motion against these midnight...

> COLLOT
>
> He's becoming relentless.

> CARNOT
>
> Distancing himself from us, you mean.

> LINDET
>
> That's enough! I will not listen to criticism of a man without his presence.

BILLAUD

I agree. Gentlemen. Robespierre has seen Danton. If he has called us at this hour, that means crisis. We must be ready to force through a decision. I say Danton must go.

CARNOT

Now wait –

COLLOT

What?

LINDET AND COLLOT

No, never!

BILLAUD

I say again, Danton must go, and together we must prevent Robespierre from leaving this chamber until he agrees to it.

CARNOT

Is he still resisting?

COLLOT

If he is, it's suspect!

BILLAUD

My God, you politicians!

COLLOT

Maybe so, Billaud, maybe so. But what's all this sudden queasiness from Robespierre? Terror's our most effective weapon – used in moderation.

LINDET

You massacred half of Lyon, you bloody murderer! This Revolution is becoming a festival of assassins!

COLLOT throws himself on LINDET and they fight, ending up on the floor.

ACT TWO

BILLAUD

That's enough!

BILLAUD and CARNOT separate the two men. They glare at each other.

CARNOT

(To COLLOT, unmoved by the fracas.) What was your point?

COLLOT glares at LINDET – who gestures at him, ferociously.

CARNOT restrains COLLOT.

COLLOT

I am asking why the sudden indecision? *(He looks at them in turn.)* What would you say of Robespierre? Brilliant leader? Has a genius for it? Well, what happens to leaders of genius?

CARNOT

They become autocrats.

COLLOT

(Impassioned)

Think! What happens to us if those two form an alliance? What happens to the Revolution, to France?

Heavy steps are heard.

COLLOT

Shhh! He's coming!

BARERE enters.

BARERE

What is it? What's the matter? *(Anxious)* Why are you all looking like that?

SAINT-JUST enters.

CARNOT

Ah! The Archangel of Terror! You're late.

SAINT-JUST

Back at school, are we?

BARERE

What's happened? Do you know?

ROBESPIERRE enters swiftly.

ROBESPIERRE

Good evening, gentlemen. I hope I haven't kept you.

COLLOT

Said the king to his ministers.

ROBESPIERRE

(Irritably.)

What's that supposed to mean?

LINDET rings bell.

CARNOT

Is there an agenda?

ROBESPIERRE

(Looks up.)

I wish to propose the following: that the arrest and trial of Georges-Jacques Danton be effected immediately.

BILLAUD

Thank God.

COLLOT

Why the rush all of a sudden?

CARNOT AND COLLOT

No, impossible.

ACT TWO

BARERE

Permission to speak?

LINDET

Barere?

BARERE

Frankly, Robespierre, your proposal terrifies me. It will take months to prepare the people.

BILLAUD
(As LINDET acknowledges his signal)
We need ten days to rally public opinion.

SAINT-JUST

Ten days for us is ten days for Danton.

ROBESPIERRE

Comrade Chairman, may I speak?

LINDET

Robespierre.

ROBESPIERRE

Saint-Just is right. Danton will attempt a coup d'état, or escape tonight. *(Looks at his watch.)* He must be in custody by three a.m.

BARERE

Tonight?

CARNOT

Are you mad?

BILLAUD AND CARNOT

Impossible, Citizen.

SAINT-JUST
(Smiles at ROBESPIERRE)
Good. You're your old self again.

COLLOT

You want us to commit suicide?

BILLAUD

Permission to speak?

LINDET

Billaud-Varenne.

BILLAUD

Danton has the bankers behind him. *(To ROBESPIERRE)* If we act prematurely, money will pour in to finance a counter revolution. You said so yourself.

Loud agreement. SAINT-JUST throws his hat across the room.

LINDET rings his bell.

BARERE

It's no use, Maxime, they won't have it!

ROBESPIERRE

(Shouts.)

I wish to speak!

BARERE

They won't have it!

BILLAUD

There'll be a panic in the Convention!

LINDET

(Rings bell.)

Be quiet, damn you!

SAINT-JUST leans over, rings the bell violently, and points to ROBESPIERRE.

ACT TWO

ROBESPIERRE
(Waits for silence.)
It is precisely because Danton has powerful backing that we must act now. At this very moment he's preparing his speech, getting ready to roar. What can we produce against that thunderous bass? My drawing room contralto? Saint-Just's tenor? Danton is a beast at bay. For the moment *(He rises)* the Committee of General Security has the power to detain Deputies. We must convene it at once.

CARNOT
But – we can't arrest Danton!

BILLAUD
(To Robespierre, irritable.)
Why the hell did you have to pick a quarrel with him?

LINDET
You cannot treat Danton as a common...

ROBESPIERRE
He will be treated exactly as any other suspect.

LINDET
But what's the indictment?

COLLOT
It will take us weeks to prepare –

ROBESPIERRE
I have the indictment here.

They crowd around, reading the indictment over one another's shoulders. ROBESPIERRE rings the bell for a SECRETARY.

Enter SECRETARY. ROBESPIERRE takes him aside.

ROBESPIERRE
We need six members of the Committee of General Security ... better make that eight. Tell them the matter is urgent.

SECRETARY
Impossible. The Committee of General Security is in session, Citizen.

ROBESPIERRE
At this time of night?

SECRETARY
Yes.

ROBESPIERRE
Well, interrupt them!

BILLAUD
Who else do we arrest? Delacroix?

Sounds of assent.

BILLAUD
Philippeaux?

LINDET
Philippeaux? No, totally innocent.

SAINT-JUST
On the contrary. His speech led the attack on the Committees.

COLLOT
Very well – who else?

BILLAUD
Camille Desmoulins?

Sudden silence. They all look at Robespierre.

ACT TWO

ROBESPIERRE

Naturally I shall abide by your decision. Should we give him a day, perhaps, to bring him to his senses?

BILLAUD

No.

SAINT-JUST

Impossible.

ROBESPIERRE

(Slight pause. Picks up pen.)

The following to be with Danton. Philippeaux.

(He writes) Delacroix...and Desmoulins.

The indictment is circulated and signed by each committee member.

CARNOT

Hardly worth leaving the building.

BARERE

(To Collot)

Will you go home?

COLLOT

No, I shall sleep here – anyway, it's raining.

BILLAUD

Lindet, you didn't sign.

LINDET

I am the Minister for Food. My responsibility is the nourishment of patriots, not their murder.

LINDET goes.

Blackout.

ACT TWO – SCENE THREE

Danton's apartment.

DELACROIX is waiting. DANTON enters.

> **DANTON**
> My God!

He laughs, excited, dashing the rain from his hat.

> **DELACROIX**
> What?

> **DANTON**
> The rain! *(Breathes.)* The first full night of spring. I could pleasure the world! My God I feel alive! Well, what do you want?

> **DELACROIX**
> The delight of your company. Have you decided?

> **DANTON**
> Decided?

> **DELACROIX**
> What's the matter with you? You must know the danger we're in!

> **DANTON**
> I've never had the slightest illusion. *(He looks out.)* Well, Paris, are you mine?

> **DELACROIX**
> They've arrested Westermann.

> **DANTON**
> When?

ACT TWO

DELACROIX

An hour ago.

DANTON

They won't touch me.

DELACROIX

Are you sure? *(He picks up his hat.)* Well, I'm leaving now. Thanks to you, I've lost the best part of the night. *(He pauses, turns at the door.)* Georges?

There is no response. He goes quickly.

DANTON

(Growls)

Pull yourself together, Danton.

CAMILLE enters swiftly.

CAMILLE

You villain. You hideous, spouting monster!

DANTON

(Turns)

In a perceptive mood, are we?

CAMILLE

I believed you!

DANTON

Bravo! On with the performance.

CAMILLE

Any performance has been by you. I thought you meant it. That we were brothers. That we were both prepared to die for a world where men could be happy, be free, could share without oppression. I'm a fool. We did the unthinkable. We killed the King. And you, Georges Danton, want to sit in his place! The most ridiculous thing of all is: I've always known it! How could I be such a fool!

DANTON
Ah, been talking to Robespierre, have we?

CAMILLE
Don't mention his name to me.

DANTON
I recognise the piety.

CAMILLE
And I thought you were both gods.

DANTON
You haven't quarreled with him? With Robespierre? You went to see him?

CAMILLE
No! He came fawning on me! Trying to trick me with his politics! Can you imagine? He won't silence The Journal that way. He's frightened of my influence ...

DANTON
You turned him away?!

CAMILLE
Of course!

DANTON
You idiot!

CAMILLE
What?

DANTON
And you don't know what you've done? You've just turned down a chance to save your life! He actually came and warned you? That you were in danger?

ACT TWO

CAMILLE

Yes.

DANTON

(Serious, he shakes his head slowly.)

Then we are finished.

CAMILLE

Finished? What do you mean?

DANTON

You listened behind the door, didn't you? You heard!

CAMILLE

But I don't understand! You defeated him!

DANTON

I made a mistake. An error. I approached him man to man. Why?! With Robespierre?!! I've condemned myself to death.

CAMILLE

But, if you didn't defeat him, why is he crawling to us?

DANTON

Is he?

Camille looks at Danton, puzzled.

CAMILLE

Defend yourself! The people of Paris are behind you ...

DANTON

(He approaches Camille.)

Do you know what I've been doing for the past two hours? Walking around the Communes. They don't even remember my name. We're lepers ... isolated.

CAMILLE

So, Robespierre...

DANTON

Was telling the truth? Oh yes.

CAMILLE

But why come to me?

DANTON

Don't you know? You're probably the only thing in the world that freak ever loved. And a painful, desperate love it's been I daresay. Where are you going?

As CAMILLE picks up his cloak.

DANTON

You're too late! You know him, he's as revengeful as the devil. He'll never forgive you.

CAMILLE

But I must at least show my gratitude for the risk he took in coming. I'll write to him...yes!

CAMILLE goes.

DANTON

He'll publish it... (*Bawls after him*)... with his comments!

He bellows with laughter, but his mood changes and he frowns. He picks up a bottle, but it is empty. He stands, motionless, his shoulders bowed, inert, head down. He looks up, a thought occurs. He crosses to the bedroom door. Knocks.

DANTON

Open the door, my dear.

ACT TWO

LOUISE
(At the door.)

What is it?

DANTON

I want to talk to you.

LOUISE
(Enters, tying her dressing gown.)

Is something wrong?

DANTON

Your family ... they're well? Your father?

LOUISE
(Surprised)

Yes, why? He hasn't been begging again?

DANTON

You must go home. At once. (*He grimaces.*)

LOUISE

Why? Are you going away? What's the matter? Are you ill?

DANTON

It's nothing. I love you. (*He grabs her.*)

LOUISE

Don't ... Please don't! Don't! I don't want to!

DANTON

I'll be very gentle. I'll hardly go inside.

LOUISE

I'm pregnant! (*She breaks away.*)

DANTON
(Sadly)

Oh, don't lie. Not now.

LOUISE

It's true.

DANTON
(Mutters)

Sod it.

He smiles at the news and starts to cuddle her. She grows agitated.

DANTON

Do you really hate me that much?

LOUISE

I don't know. Yes.

DANTON

Why? I've never done you any harm.

LOUISE

What? You bought me like a dog on a string. A bargain! You couldn't stop smiling.

DANTON

Louise...

LOUISE

What pleased you most? That I was terrified?

DANTON

No! My darling, I had no idea. I thought that once you'd enjoyed love... once you'd experienced it...

LOUISE
(A shriek of laughter.)

You think anyone goes with you from choice? Does any girl go with an older man – for pleasure?

ACT TWO

He is mesmerised by her hate.

> LOUISE
>
> *(Hisses, close)*
>
> He'll beat you. How do I know? You're like my father. The more he's beaten, the more he boasts. Every time I hear you slandering Monsieur Robespierre I know he is beating you, and I get down on my knees and I thank God for it!

She cringes as he closes on her. But he turns away, controlling himself.

> DANTON
>
> *(Mutters)*
>
> Shut up or I'll kill you. (*He turns and looks at her, fascinated.*) My God. She's happy. The first time we've seen her smile. Oh, my dear, you should have kept your mouth shut! I was going to let them butcher me. I'd had enough.

He approaches her. She retreats.

> DANTON
>
> You think a Robespierre can win? Can beat a Danton?

He grimaces fearsomely, his face close. She winces.

> DANTON
>
> You think I can't turn them back ... that rabble ...in a night? I'll have Paris in my hand before the cocks crow.

Again, the frightening grimace, making her shudder away from him. Then a loud knocking. They both freeze.

DANTON feels a sudden wave of nausea, reels slightly, and tries to control the sensation with a dreadful smile.

DANTON

What? Already? Impossible.

He looks at Louise who responds with a small, stiff smile.

DANTON

(Shouts at door)

Are you looking for Georges Danton? Here I am! Come up, damn you – as long as there's breath in these lungs, you're wasting your time!

LOUISE

Boasting again, Georges?

He turns on her and kisses her with a mix of rage and desire. A YOUNG OFFICER enters with FOUR SOLDIERS.

DANTON

(Into her hair)

As for you, oh you ... you won't be rid of me. Only death will free you from me now. Two days ... I'll be back. Two days!

YOUNG OFFICER

Citizen Danton?

DANTON

Of course, who the hell do you think it is?

YOUNG OFFICER

Georges-Jacques Danton, I arrest you in the name of the Convention, the Revolution, and the people of France. Here is the warrant.

DANTON brushes it away so violently that the officer has to bend and pick it up.

DANTON

I know, I know. My dear, my hat ...

ACT TWO

LOUISE does not move. He picks it up himself.

DANTON
Glorious night, I shan't need my coat. Is it still raining?

YOUNG OFFICER
(Embarrassed by the friendly question.)
Ah ... no, sir.

DANTON
'Citizen' – 'Citizen' – no 'sirs' here ... You're a good revolutionary, aren't you?

He laughs. No-one responds. They wait for him to move, so he steps forward, and the soldiers wheel to follow him off.

LOUISE
Excuse me.

They all turn. The OFFICER steps back for her to make her farewells. She does not move.

LOUISE
Where do you wish me to send his effects?

DANTON
My wife means my belongings, for the next few days.

OFFICER
To the ... ah ... Luxembourg Palace, Citizeness.

LOUISE crosses, picks up Danton's coat and holds it out to him. He takes it, smiles gaily, and gives her a hearty kiss, with a smile at the men.

DANTON
Thank you, my dear!

She moves away brusquely. He bows with brief, ironic gallantry.

DANTON

Right, friends, are we ready?

He wheels and strides out purposefully, followed meekly by his young captors. LOUISE watches them go. She waits for the sound of the door below, then crosses to the window and looks down into the courtyard until they are out of sight.

She comes back to the centre of the room and remains for a moment, without expression. Then she lifts the shawl on her shoulders, picks up the candelabrum, and returns to the bedroom.

Fade to black.

END OF ACT TWO

ACT THREE

ACT THREE - SCENE ONE

The Convention.

An atmosphere of noise and tension as members enter.

> FRERON
> *(Calls)*
>
> You mean you saw them being taken?
>
> LECOINTRE
>
> Who ... who?
>
> MERLIN
>
> When?
>
> LECOINTRE
>
> What names?

They converse together urgently.

> PANIS
> *(Second Group)*
>
> No, I don't believe it!
>
> COURTOIS
>
> They wouldn't dare!
>
> MERLIN
> *(Calls to Panis Group)*
>
> What's happened?
>
> PANIS
>
> We don't know!

COURTOIS

It's the usual rumour!

A CONVENTION SECRETARY enters quickly.

COURTOIS
(*To SECRETARY*)

Is it true? Have there been arrests?

He pulls the SECRETARY to one side. Listens, then jumps on a chair.

COURTOIS

Citizens! Citizens! Desmoulins has been arrested!
They've arrested Camille!

Sensation.

BOURDON and LEGENDRE rush in and are surrounded.

BOURDON

Please, please ... I may be taken at any moment!

LEGENDRE

We're all at risk. The government of France is being threatened, friends!

MERLIN

They want to murder us all!

LECOINTRE

Citizens, are we to give way to Terror? (*Shouts*) I say, no dictatorship! Revolution for the people by the people!

He begins to sing 'La Marseillaise.'

They all sing as BILLAUD, COLLOT, CARNOT and BARERE enter, also singing, several phrases behind.

As the singing ends, TWO USHERS enter and bang the floor with halberds. TALLIEN, the chairman, follows them formally.

ACT THREE

He pauses, consults the CONVENTION SECRETARY, nods, and ascends to his seat. There is a rush to the rostrum to speak.

TALLIEN

The Convention is now in session!

LEGENDRE

(Shouts)

Comrades of the Convention – Citizen Chairman, I wish to speak!

TALLIEN waves assent and LEGENDRE ascends the rostrum.

ROBESPIERRE and SAINT-JUST enter, and stand apart.

LEGENDRE

We hear, to our amazement and disbelief, that four of our colleagues – four members of this house – have been arrested! *(Noise.)* And that one – and that one of them – one of them.... *(Above the noise)* Citizens! Citizens! The integrity of our fellow revolutionary and patriot Danton is beyond reproach. I vouch for it with my life!

Applause.

LEGENDRE

I move ... I move that those who have been arrested are permitted to answer any charges from the floor of this chamber!

Roar of assent. He motions for silence.

LEGENDRE

Only then can we judge whether personal feelings...(*He leans forward, wild-eyed*) Envy – envy, friends, is the motive behind these disgraceful arrests. Are we to submit to this stain on the Revolution?

Fervent applause as he leaves the dais. ROBESPIERRE pushes his way to the rostrum and refuses to be dislodged. SAINT-JUST is at his side.

> ROBESPIERRE
> *(Shrill shout)*
> I request the right to speak!

More pushing and shoving.

> ROBESPIERRE
> Citizen Legendre!

> CONVENTION SECRETARY
> *(Sing-song, at a nod from TALLIEN)*
> Robespierre to speak!

Reluctantly, the others fall back. ROBESPIERRE steps up briskly to the rostrum. A hush.

> ROBESPIERRE
> Citizens!

There is pandemonium.

> VOICES
> Danton! Where is Danton? We want Danton! Get down! Stand down! Down with tyrants! Down with the Committees! Where is Danton? Danton!

COURTOIS points at ROBESPIERRE.

> COURTOIS
> *(Roars)*
> Down with the dictator!

This sobers the House. Robespierre has to wait, but the House subsides to a gloomy silence.

ACT THREE

> ROBESPIERRE
> *(Sighs)*
> It's a long time, gentlemen, since we began our sitting with such a display of temper. There is obviously a matter of great importance to be discussed.

> BOURDON
> *(Yells)*
> Who sent the Hébertistes to their deaths? And who's next?

Noise.

> ROBESPIERRE
> Today – today we shall see what we value more. The Republic – the Republic...or the individual.

> FRERON
> We'll see if you deserve to stand there, tyrant!

> ROBESPIERRE
> I will raise that point too. In a moment. (*Waits for silence.*) Citizens Legendre demands that the accused be tried before this chamber.

Shouts of assent.

> ROBESPIERRE
> But when...but when (*Waits*)... But when we arrested the Hébertistes...was this requested? Do you wish to accord to those now under arrest concessions which you have denied to others? On what grounds? Citizen Legendre mentions the name of Danton. He knows the names of the others but mentions only Danton. Why? Is this the name of someone especially privileged? If Citizen Legendre believes this then it is a mistake which we must

correct in him. There are no privileged people here.
Privilege is what we seek to abolish.

Cheers for and against him. Murmurs.

ROBESPIERRE

Perhaps we should rather be wondering why any man would want – would dare – to assume for himself the title of The Man of the Tenth of August. The tenth of August, 1792, was the work of a United Will!

Cheers. ROBESPIERRE gazes at the ceiling.

ROBESPIERRE

Besides, Danton's participation was by no means prominent. However, when the battle was won, who was there, ready and eager to gather the laurels for himself?

Cheers of agreement and shouts of dissent.

ROBESPIERRE

I am the first to agree that Danton has merits.

Some cheering.

ROBESPIERRE

What of it? Everyone here has achieved greatness. I look around this chamber and I see the faces of heroes – here – here – here ... What of it? You claim no right to distinction ...to prizes. None of us is here to claim privilege. For anything. *(He looks around with a keen gaze.)* Perhaps if the career of Danton were without blemish but ... *(Against rising sound, he raises his voice)* ... but it has been, in the main, no more than a succession of crimes against the state!

Uproar.

ACT THREE

> ROBESPIERRE
> So much so that, in the case of Danton, the demand for special treatment is no more than impudence – and a contemptuous defiance of the law! Let us see if members of the Convention have the strength, the moral purpose to topple that clay Colossus or whether they will allow themselves to be dragged down with him and thus deprive France of her lawful government. We shall see.

Applause. Shouts for both sides.

> LECOINTRE
> To hear the accused from this floor is not privilege but simple justice!

Applause.

> ROBESPIERRE
> Justice? You mean that you have no trust in the procedure and actions of our constitutionally elected Revolutionary Tribunal? Citizen, you insult the state that we have created!

Applause, stamping.

> VOICES
> Bravo! Bravo, Maxime! Long live Robespierre! Long live the Committees! Long Live the Revolution!

MERLIN jumps to his feet.

> MERLIN
> Can't you see? Can't you see it'll be our turn next!

> COURTOIS
> Have you all gone mad? If Danton falls we're none of us safe!

ROBESPIERRE

These two gentlemen by their statements appear to have confessed their guilt.

MERLIN

What did you say?

ROBESPIERRE

Since the Assembly appears to accord full confidence in the Committees and the Tribunal, those who publicly flout them are betrayed as criminals.

COURTOIS

Robespierre, if you accomplish this vile work of envy and ambition, then I tell you this. The fall of Danton will crush you to dust.

COURTOIS and MERLIN leave.

ROBESPIERRE

(After a silence.)

An argument, may I say, gentlemen, which is far from novel. If by some mystic law the destruction of a criminal should bring about my ruin, what of it? Are we to allow private danger to inhibit decision?

Silence. He leans forward on the rostrum.

ROBESPIERRE

Gentlemen, why are we here? Why are we prepared to withstand every assault that the rest of the world seeks to launch against us? *(His voice trembles).* I will tell you. We are here to change everything. We seek, simply, to begin again.

Murmurs of agreement.

ACT THREE

ROBESPIERRE

We seek to create a new society. A society based on the Greek notion of democracy. To some, a new idea. To many, frightening. What does it mean? Where will it lead? To chaos? *(Slight pause.)* Or to justice and freedom for all? I say that the future of the whole world lies with us ... Here ... Now! And most particularly with those of us sitting in this Chamber.

Silence.

ROBESPIERRE

Citizens, I ask you to embrace the principles of democracy. To embrace the notion of personal freedom for all. No man is born a slave – only another man makes him so!

Applause. He waits for silence.

ROBESPIERRE

What is our task? Firstly, to survive. Secondly, to establish a humane, a decent, a self-respecting and virtuous society. A society without hierarchy. Without privilege. A world in which personal fulfilment is accepted as an inalienable human right.

A murmur of doubt.

ROBESPIERRE

You think that impossible? Why? Think of the waste! Seas – oceans of energy – lost in beings beaten down by hunger, want, lack of education, the bare means of survival. *(He leans forward.)* We have the means to unlock that energy. To release it. Channel it. Allow it to swell over the face of the earth like a newly discovered element ... a new oxygen! Here – now – for the first

> time in the history of the world, we ... here ... now ...
> have the opportunity, the challenge, the chance to
> change the world – for the world – for the peoples of the
> world – everywhere! Liberty!

Cheers

> ROBESPIERRE
>
> Equality!

Cheers

> ROBESPIERRE
>
> Fraternity!

Louder cheers. He lifts his hand for silence, and looks around at his listeners.

> ROBESPIERRE
>
> Must it all go to waste? All the courage that
> created this great revolution be squandered? For
> criminality?

The murmurs begin to swell.

> ROBESPIERRE
> *(Shouts in a high shriek)*
> I say no!! Never! Not while a revolutionary heart lives
> and breathes in this Chamber. The work of our two
> great Committees must survive!

Cheers and applause.

Shouts for Robespierre. His manner changes. He speaks briskly in a matter-of-fact way.

> ROBESPIERRE
>
> Citizen Chairman, I move that the order for the arrest
> of Citizens Danton, Desmoulins, Philippeaux and

Delacroix, together with the arrest of the thief Fabre
D'Eglantine, and the royalist Herault de Seychelles be
confirmed, and that the motion of Citizen Legendre be
rejected.

Shouts of agreement.

> TALLIEN
>
> *(Shouts)*
>
> Who votes for the motion. Who votes for the motion?

Almost all rise.

> TALLIEN
>
> Motion passed by majority vote.

SAINT-JUST leans over, asking for permission to speak. LEGENDRE rises. ROBESPIERRE, exhausted, sits.

> LEGENDRE
>
> *(Tense)*
>
> Robespierre ... You must understand – I had no
> intention of putting Danton before the common
> good ...

> ROBESPIERRE
>
> I never dreamed it for a moment, Citizen.

> BOURDON
>
> *(Rushes to dais.)*
>
> Gentlemen! I was a victim of Danton's criminality! I
> have realised my grave error! As proof of my trust,
> I propose to issue the decree of indictment against
> Delacroix, Philippeaux, Desmoulins ...and ... *(He
> stumbles badly)* ... and Danton.

Applause. As it dies away, there is a solitary burst of laughter. SAINT-JUST, on his way to the dais, pauses and turns.

> TALLIEN
> *(Amid hostile murmurs)*
> Citizen, why are you laughing?

> PANIS
> *(Rises, his eyes roving nervously.)*
> I apologise to the Assembly. It is a nervous
> manifestation... *(He bites his lip)*...
> Especially...especially in solemn...in solemn
> moments.

He stifles his laughter in a handkerchief amid murmuring.

SAINT-JUST ascends the dais.

> TALLIEN
> *(Depressed)*
> Who votes against Bourdon's motion?

Silence.

> TALLIEN
> The decree of indictment is passed by acclamation.

ROBESPIERRE nods to SAINT-JUST who raises his hand for silence.

> SAINT-JUST
> I have here detailed reports of the criminal activities
> of the accused as compiled by officers of the
> Committee of General Security. The document is in
> seventeen sections, each dealing with a separate area
> of indictment. Thirty-one prosecution witnesses are
> here present and one hundred and twenty-six will be
> available for cross-examination before the Tribunal
> as required. Item One...

Blackout.

ACT THREE

ACT THREE - SCENE TWO

The Luxembourg Palace arranged as a prison, with camp beds and a barred window.

PHILIPPEAUX is sitting on his bed, reading. He looks up at CAMILLE, who is by the window, weeping quietly.

PHILIPPEAUX
Desmoulins! Are you not embarrassed to break down like this before strangers?

CAMILLE
How can I help it on such a day? It's April ... Germinal! (*He leans against the window.*) I want to taste it ... smell it! How can I behind bars?

PHILIPPEAUX
If you go on like this, I shall ask to be moved.

CAMILLE
No please – I shall go mad on my own.

PHILIPPEAUX
Try to control yourself.

CAMILLE
How? I tell you, he walked away. Crossed me out!

He breaks down again. PHILIPPEAUX reaches for the bell.

CAMILLE
No please! Sweet Jesus! (*Masters himself.*) All I wanted was to tell him. That I knew. That he risked his own life trying to save me. He was speaking the truth. As he's always done.

He sobs. PHILIPPEAUX watches him in silence.

CAMILLE

I am sorry .... I've lost the respect of the only honest man I've ever known apart from you. Please, you must help me, or I'm finished.

PHILIPPEAUX

But my dear Desmoulins, you are finished. In five days' we shall all be dead. (*They stare at each other.*) Try to accept it. You'll find that it helps.

CAMILLE

You're lying! They can't kill us!

PHILIPPEAUX

Of course, they can. This will be a political trial. We have clashed with the two great committees. They are the stronger – ergo, we shall perish.

CAMILLE

But I don't want to die, I want to live! It's my life – I've a right to it!

PHILIPPEAUX

Only so long as you can preserve that right.

They turn as CHAUMETTE, HERAULT, THE COMTE and VICOMTE D'ESTAING enter.

HERAULT

(*Young and handsome, well-dressed.*)
Greetings in the name of the Widow Guillotine!

PHILIPPEAUX

Gentlemen, there must be some mistake. This is a private cell.

Laughter.

ACT THREE

HERAULT

We bribed the guard!

VICOMTE

Who is this gentleman?

CHAUMETTE

Why, it's Philippeaux. I'm amazed to see you here, sir. The revolution devours its own!

Sees CAMILLE.

CHAUMETTE

Camille! Is it true? The rumour that Danton himself has been arrested?

CAMILLE sways as if he is going to faint. The royalists help him.

CAMILLE

Thank you, friends.

COMTE

Not at all, my dear sir.

PHILIPPEAUX

Gentlemen, allow me to introduce you – Camille Desmoulins – the Comte, and the Vicomte D'Estaing.

CAMILLE

(Recoils as if stung. Then ...)

Well ... companions in misfortune ...

They shake hands awkwardly.

To the shock of those present, DANTON sweeps in with DELACROIX, LAFLOTTE, WESTERMANN and FABRE, who is clearly ill.

CHAUMETTE

Danton's here!

VICOMTE
Merciful Jesus!

All but the royalists embrace.

CHAUMETTE
So, it's true!

HERAULT
My God, Georges, how is it possible?

FABRE
Now we know the revolution is dead.

COMTE
(Apart)
I suggest we're civil. After all, Danton has not been unfriendly to us.

VICOMTE
Yes, but one can hardly shake hands with hirelings.

HERAULT
We've been watching your struggles, gentlemen. Courage! Robespierre won't outlast the flowers of May!

CHAUMETTE
Don't you mean Prairial?

DELACROIX
Call it what you will. Either way, our bones will be bubbling in quicklime by then.

DANTON
That's enough of that. Chairs! A chair for Fabre!

CAMILLE
(Offers FABRE a seat.)
Philippe?

ACT THREE

> FABRE
> *(Surprised.)*
> Oh hullo, Camille. Are we speaking again?

> CAMILLE
> *(Glares at DANTON)*
> I've had my eyes opened.

> DANTON
> Gentlemen. At eight o'clock tomorrow morning, most of us will be taken to the Conciergerie.

CAMILLE begins to shake. HERAULT turns away and throws up. He recovers with an apologetic smile.

> DANTON
> And brought to trial in the next few days.

> FABRE
> My God.

> CHAUMETTE
> Cowards!

> DANTON
> What's the matter with you all? Our hands may be tied but we still have our lungs! They haven't won yet, and if we fight they won't!

> CHAUMETTE
> Fight? How?

> DANTON
> Gentlemen, who are the government – these so-called judges? Yesterday's scum!

> DELACROIX
> And so incompetent that we are the prisoners and they are the jailors.

DANTON

What's the matter with you? Wetting your britches again? Fight, damn you, we're not dead yet!

COMTE

Danton is right!

VICOMTE

Father!

LAFLOTTE

Yes, bravo.

CAMILLE

Georges ... do you think we have a chance?

PHILIPPEAUX

Don't delude yourself, Desmoulins.

They all turn towards him.

PHILIPPEAUX

None of us will get out of this.

WESTERMANN

(Glowers at Philippeaux.)

Good God, man!

HERAULT

What sort of talk is that?

LAFLOTTE

Throw him out! We don't need spies!

PHILIPPEAUX

(Rises and closes his book.)

You are mistaken, sir.

LAFLOTTE

How do we know? Out!

ACT THREE

He forces PHILIPPEAUX to the door.

> **COMTE**
> *(Discreetly, of Laflotte)*
>
> Who is that gentleman?
>
> **DELACROIX**
>
> I don't know. He'd better leave too.
>
> **LAFLOTTE**
> *(Bows.)*
>
> Laflotte – ex-government envoy to Venice.
>
> **DELACROIX**
> *(Grabs him.)*
>
> Out!
>
> **CAMILLE**
>
> Oh, please stop!

DELACROIX lets go of LAFLOTTE.

> **FABRE**
>
> How do we fight?
>
> **DANTON**
>
> I'll tell you, gentlemen. (*He gestures, and they group around him.*) A political trial is not a trial. It is a duel. So, it is as a duel that we conduct this case. Attack, attack ... always attack! And never forget. There is only one body with the power to judge both parties. I speak of the people. So. In the Tribunal, before the people, we counter every accusation, and we accuse. We threaten revelation – persistently – and we do that until the Tribunal is forced to adjourn ...
>
> **DELACROIX**
>
> Or until they pass sentence without trial.

CHAUMETTE
Pass sentence, on Danton? They wouldn't dare!

LAFLOTTE
They'd be slaughtered in their seats!

CAMILLE
He's right. Once the galleries hear Georges –

DANTON
My voice is our talisman. The moment I open my mouth ... Believe me, the people of France will stand with us as soon as they hear my roar.

DELACROIX
Bellow as long as you like, there are still charges to be answered. You really think you can talk yourself out of this?

HERAULT
Rousing the public, damn risky, Georges ...

WESTERMANN
Bloody galleries, bloody unpredictable. Could go the other way.

DANTON
Precisely. Which is why we refuse to answer charges until our defence witnesses have been heard!

WESTERMANN
Defence witnesses?

CHAUMETTE
Who will dare?

DANTON
There'll be those who'll speak for me. (*He laughs.*) Believe me, it'll be in their interest!

ACT THREE

HERAULT
You mean, once they've testified on our behalf...

CHAUMETTE
But the Tribunal won't want that. They'll try to prevent it.

DANTON
In front of the people?

HERAULT
Yes, if they refuse, they'll be forced to let us go.

DANTON
And if they do produce them?

WESTERMANN
We've won.

DANTON
We've won.

HERAULT
This could work...

CAMILLE
Oh, it will. It must!

FABRE
It's a chance.

DANTON
Gentlemen. The release of you all is my sacred task and duty, and I intend to fulfil that solemn obligation.

COMTE
(Shaking his hand.)
My dear Monsieur!

VICOMTE

You give us hope after two long years of despair.

DANTON

But we must unite. Only together can we win!

VICOMTE

Absolutely. We must dissolve all mistrust!

DANTON

Old enemies, new friends!

COMTE

We have many allies on the outside.

DANTON

Good. Our connections must form a league at once. Chaumette, take down a letter to Camille's wife.

CAMILLE

For God's sake, you can't involve Lucille. Think of the child!

DANTON

Rubbish – she's perfectly safe – the most popular woman in Paris.

HERAULT

We must list names...

CHAUMETTE

It'll be another Tenth of August!

LAFLOTTE

Let me take the letter. I know one of the guards –

DELACROIX

I'd advise you all not to get excited.

ACT THREE

GUARD
(At the door, fearful, to Camille)
Citizen – you have a visitor!

CAMILLE
Who? My wife? *(He rises, excited.)*

DANTON
(Looks up)
Lucille, where?

GUARD
No, please, you mustn't say anything. You're supposed to be in separate cells. *(To CAMILLE)* He thinks you're alone.Gentlemen, quiet please, I beg of you!

PHILIPPEAUX enters.

PHILIPPEAUX
Desmoulins. Robespierre is waiting to see you.

A shocked silence.

PHILIPPEAUX
Down the corridor to the right.

He crosses and sits as CAMILLE gazes, anguished, at DANTON.

PHILIPPEAUX
Hurry up, man. He's waiting!

CAMILLE
(Half-howls)
Georges! ... please! What am I to do?!

PHILIPPEAUX
Go, you fool!

WESTERMANN
Save your skin – go home.

FABRE

Who's stopping you?

DELACROIX

Why die with us? Get out while you can.

DANTON rises and approaches CAMILLE. He bows lightly and waves CAMILLE to the door with a smile.

DANTON

Adieu Camille!

CAMILLE stands, immobile. DANTON regards him with mocking defiance.

CAMILLE

(Without taking his eyes from DANTON)
Tell the gentleman that I have no wish to see him.

GUARD

I can't say that, sir!

PHILIPPEAUX

Go, damn you!

CAMILLE shakes his head.

PHILIPPEAUX

Don't you want to live?

CAMILLE

Yes, of course. But I also understand the meaning of loyalty.

COMTE

Bravo, Monsieur!

GUARD

But what am I to say, Citizen?

ACT THREE

CAMILLE

Say what you please! Tell him I'm ill – dead! Oh, suit yourself. I shall not see him.

FABRE

Tell him Camille is not receiving today!

Laughter.

GUARD

But...

The GUARD stands there, trembling. More laughter as he scuttles off. DANTON claps CAMILLE on the shoulder as the rest applaud.

DANTON

Done like a man! Right – to business.

DANTON moves apart, followed by all but PHILIPPEAUX and CAMILLE.

CAMILLE

What else could I have done? Honour demanded it. It was the only possible thing.

PHILIPPEAUX

My friend, you lack the discernment, it seems, not only to choose friends, but also to look out for your own survival.

PHILIPPEAUX closes his book, folds his clothes primly, using his jacket for a pillow. The light begins to go.

CAMILLE throws himself down on his bed with a painful groan. The others disperse.

CAMILLE

Oh God! I wish I were dead!

Fade out.

ACT THREE – SCENE THREE

The Library at DANTON's house.

LOUISE DANTON is writing letters. The SOUND of the Tocsin. She shudders, then seals a letter. A KNOCK. She rises.

LUCILLE DESMOULINS enters.

> LUCILLE
> I wish to see Madame Danton!

> LOUISE
> I am Louise Danton.

> LUCILLE
> No, I mean the Deputy's wife. The wife of Georges Danton.

> LOUISE
> Yes?

> LUCILLE
> You are Louise Danton? How old are you?

> LOUISE
> I am sixteen.

> LUCILLE
> Forgive me! Please, I must speak to you!

> LOUISE
> I'm afraid there is no point. None at all.

> LUCILLE
> Oh, but I beg of you ...

> LOUISE
> I'm sorry.

ACT THREE

LUCILLE

But together we can save them!

LOUISE moves away. LUCILLE grabs her arm.

LUCILLE

We can! We must!

Pause.

LOUISE turns, coldly.

LOUISE

There is something you can do.

LUCILLE

Then you will join us?

LOUISE

No. I suggest that you write to Monsieur Robespierre. Tell him that your husband is disillusioned with Danton. Sees through him. Knows him as a criminal, an embezzler, and an enemy of the people.

LUCILLE

(Shocked)

But . . .

LOUISE

You must say that he cannot bear the thought of dying without its being publicly known that he is a genuine and loving supporter of Maximilian Robespierre. On no account must he ask for mercy – that is important. There is a chance – just a chance – that your husband may be saved. And please don't mention my name.

LEGENDRE appears.

LOUISE

Ah, Citizen Legendre.

LUCILLE

(Grabs him by the arm.)

Citizen Legendre, you're Danton's friend ... Kill Robespierre. Kill him as he leaves his house. There's no-one about then.

LEGENDRE

Ah, ladies! Upset, are we? Don't worry your little heads. Between ourselves, the Convention's made a pretty good fool of itself – carried away by Robespierre as usual. Don't fret. Danton will set the record straight. The Tribunal won't dare touch him.

LUCILLE

We're organizing a league in support. May we count on ...

LEGENDRE

Citizeness! Have some sense! Run about the city like this, you'll have every spy in Paris in your tail!

LUCILLE

(To LOUISE)

Will you help?

LOUISE

(Shakes her head.)

Your plan is silly.

LUCILLE looks from one to the other, as LOUISE and LEGENDRE stand side by side. And she misinterprets.

LUCILLE

Oh! I see! ... I see!

ACT THREE

She recoils from them and rushes away.

> **LEGENDRE**
> I'm glad to see that Madame Danton is as sensible as she is beautiful.

> **LOUISE**
> What did you want, Monsieur Legendre?

> **LEGENDRE**
> Thought I'd call. See how you were. Wife of a colleague...

> **LOUISE**
> *(Suddenly exhausted)*
> Thank you.

She sits.

> **LEGENDRE**
> *(Sits beside her.)*
> I wish the brave little Madame Lucille every success – with all my heart. Still, let's keep our heads on our shoulders, eh? (*He closes on her.*) Is there anything you need?

> **LOUISE**
> Thank you, no.

> **LEGENDRE**
> It's not going to be easy without fat Georges to look after you. (*He pats her hand.*) I'm not without influence.

> **LOUISE**
> Yes.

> **LEGENDRE**
> After all, I am your husband's friend.

LOUISE

Friend?

LEGENDRE

(Genial)

His survivor, I hope! *(Laughs, and touches her arm.)*
My advice to you, my dear, is to sit very, very still.

Fade to black.

ACT THREE – SCENE FOUR

The Vestibule of the Tribunal.

CITIZENS crowd the doors, which are guarded by an USHER. As the doors open, we hear DANTON'S VOICE.

DANTON

(Offstage)

... any honest man take seriously the lies they've been spreading? Let them dare to stand before me and repeat their shameful slanders to my face!

CITIZEN 1

That's it, Danton!

DANTON

(Offstage)

Let them produce our witnesses ... we'll expose these enemies of the people, so that they'll leap up the steps of the Widow Guillotine for shame!

Sound of the BELL. Sound cuts off as FOUQUIER enters and closes the door.

ACT THREE

FOUQUIER

(Snarls to TRIBUNAL USHER)

What are these people doing here? Get rid of them!

USHER

But Citizen ...

FOUQUIER

Get them out. No-one's allowed in the corridors!

CITIZEN 2

There's no room inside!

CITIZEN 3

Who's he?

CITIZEN 2

Fouquier, Public Prosecutor!

CITIZEN 1

No need to take it out on us!

CITIZEN 4

Just because they're making a fool of you in there ...

CITIZEN 3

What about open hearings? Is this a new decree?

CITIZEN 4

We can stand on the roof if we want!

FOUQUIER

Can you? Can you?

He throws them out as BILLAUD and VADIER enter, and approach the door to the Tribunal.

BILLAUD

(As they cross)

Fouquier's a bungler. Ah, Fouquier! Well?

FOUQUIER

Danton's refusing to answer charges without witnesses.

He opens the door to demonstrate. They listen.

DANTON

(Off)

... guilty of treachery – and Fouquier-Tinville ... as we all know well ... is an honourable man!

Offstage laughter.

FOUQUIER

Damn him. That mad bull is making a fool of me!

BILLAUD

That mad bull is being heard by the whole of Paris!

VADIER

You must silence him immediately.

FOUQUIER

How? Tell me how?

VADIER

Don't ask me, that's your job!

FOUQUIER

In that case, mind your own business!

BILLAUD

Fouquier ...

FOUQUIER

They've a right to their damn witnesses!

ACT THREE

BILLAUD
(Levelly)

I am instructing you– on behalf of the Convention.
Finish it.

FOUQUIER

Tell me how! Tell me what to do, that's all!

HERMANN, in judge's robes, enters through the door, holding a sheaf of pages. Laughter is heard and cheering.

HERMANN

The list of defence witnesses demanded by the
accused.

Gives the papers to FOUQUIER.

HERMANN

Please! – I can't hold them in there! I shall have to
suspend the proceedings!

FOUQUIER

It is not our decision. The Convention must decide. Let
the Convention decide!

He thrusts the list at BILLAUD.

BILLAUD

Very well. (*To VADIER, thrusting the list at him*)
Send a letter to the Committee of Public Safety. Tell
them I advise, most urgently, against the witnesses.
(*To FOUQUIER*) Now, for God' sake get in there,
Fouquier, and do your job!

FOUQUIER

All right, all right, all right!

They go separately.

Fade Out.

ACT THREE – SCENE FIVE

ROBESPIERRE at home. Night.

He has dozed off. ELEONORE enters.

> ELEONORE
>
> I've made you some soup.

> ROBESPIERRE
>
> No! *(He adjusts to his normal voice.)* I'm going mad. I'm sorry.

> ELEONORE
>
> You haven't eaten for twenty-four hours.

> ROBESPIERRE
>
> Please. Not now.

> ELEONORE
>
> *(Bursts out)*
>
> Have some concern for me! A year ago, you were one step away from the guillotine, but you didn't look like this! Eat!

She stands over him, puts a napkin around his neck. He picks up the spoon like an obedient child.

> ELEONORE
>
> Thank you.

ELEONORE steps back and watches him fervently as he takes a mouthful, then puts the spoon down.

> ELEONORE
>
> Five years of suffering and struggle – and for what?!

ROBESPIERRE picks up his spoon but suddenly panics.

ACT THREE

ROBESPIERRE

God, what time is it?

A KNOCK. He springs to his feet.

ROBESPIERRE

Come in, come in – (*to ELEONORE*) – Excuse me.

ELEONORE leaves with the tray, passing FOUQUIER as BARERE enters and bows.

BARERE

Good-evening.

ROBESPIERRE
(Fixing his buttons calmly.)
What news? Ah, Monsieur Fouquier, we meet in private for the first time, if I'm not mistaken. Do sit down. (*Finishes his toilette with finicky precision.*) Barere, good to see you. Please suggest a double watch on the prisons. With Danton's arrest, there will be an increase in counter-revolutionary activities. What may I do for you, gentlemen?

FOUQUIER

The trial is disintegrating into chaos. Danton refuses to respect our authority. He's turning the court into a circus.

ROBESPIERRE

Very well. Bring the trial to an end.

FOUQUIER

How?!

ROBESPIERRE

That's your affair.

FOUQUIER

We are bound by the process of law. He's saying what he likes.

ROBESPIERRE

(Comfortably)

Deprive him of his right to speak.

FOUQUIER

If we do that there will be a riot.

ROBESPIERRE

Then I suggest that you pass the death sentence first thing in the morning.

FOUQUIER

There is another matter. The letter containing their demand for witnesses was sent to the Committee of Public Safety. *(Turns to BARERE.)*

BARERE

We appear not to have received it, Citizen Robespierre.

ROBESPIERRE

It's here. In my pocket. *(Smiles.)* I embezzled it.

BARERE

Why?

FOUQUIER

You took it upon yourself...

ROBESPIERRE

If the Convention chooses to reply it will refuse the request. I understand your difficulties, Monsieur Fouquier, but there are certain considerations which take precedence over legality. Thus, if you consider the destruction of the criminal Danton to be a violation of the law, then you are instructed to violate the law.

FOUQUIER

I am a public prosecutor, not an executioner in your service.

ROBESPIERRE

Not in my service but, in the service of revolutionary justice, an executioner is precisely what you are. We are delivering the enemies of the Republic into your hands not to be judged, but to be removed.

BARERE

But you haven't seen what's happening! He's inciting the whole of Paris against us!

ROBESPIERRE

(Closes on him like a snake.)

One more treasonable word like that and you will be sent to prison from this room. *(To FOUQUIER)* and that goes for you! Vadier has the warrants in his pocket.

FOUQUIER glares at him.

BARERE

(Whispers)

Maxime...Please! The courts can't function under Terror.

ROBESPIERRE

Can't they... oh, can't they? We'll see about that! *(He looks at his watch.)* Dammit, I'm late. Have I made myself clear?

FOUQUIER

(Snarls)

Oh perfectly.

ROBESPIERRE

Then may I depend on your cooperation?

BARERE

Yes.

ROBESPIERRE

Splendid.

He shakes FOUQUIER's hand cordially.

FOUQUIER

Let's hope there's not an assassin out there waiting to plunge a dagger in your heart – for the sake of the revolution.

ROBESPIERRE

(Laughs)

Let's hope not.

He goes.

BARERE

I wish I shared that hope, but I don't.

FOUQUIER

What?

BARERE

Not any longer.

FOUQUIER turns on him.

FOUQUIER

What did you say, Citizen?

ACT THREE

> BARERE
>
> Nothing, nothing I assure you!
>
> FOUQUIER
>
> You were speaking of the safety of Citizen Robespierre.
>
> BARERE
>
> *(Gabbles)*
>
> We must protect him, all of us ... with our blood if necessary!

He backs away from FOUQUIER's ferocious approach, then doubles up with cramp, and messes himself, groaning loudly with pain.

> FOUQUIER
>
> *(A handkerchief to his nose.)*
>
> Oh, for God's sake!

He moves off irritably.

> BARERE
>
> I'm sorry. I shall need another pair of trousers.
>
> FOUQUIER
>
> *(With a sneer.)*
>
> We keep a supply, Citizen.

He looks at BARERE contemptuously and goes. BARERE hobbles after him.

Blackout.

ACT THREE – SCENE SIX

The Conciergerie. Night.

PHILIPPEAUX reading by candlelight. CAMILLE is standing on a table, looking out of the window.

DELACROIX, WESTERMANN, FABRE and HERAULT are lying on bunks.

>   WESTERMANN
>
> Anyone awake?
>
>   DELACROIX
>   *(Getting up)*
> Is anyone asleep, do you mean?

CAMILLE jumps down with a crash, making him jump.

>   DELACROIX
>
> Don't do that!
>
>   FABRE
>
> For God's sake!
>
>   CAMILLE
>
> My apologies.
>
>   DELACROIX
>   *(Murderous smile)*
> We're all a little jumpy tonight.
>
>   FABRE
>
> It's because we're being tortured by hope.
>
>   WESTERMANN
>
> Three days! How much longer can it go on?
>
>   FABRE
>
> We must contain ourselves. The Tribunal is afraid to move. It could last for weeks.
>
>   PHLIPPEAUX
>
> You're wrong. This trial will be over tomorrow. We shall all be condemned to death.

ACT THREE

HERAULT

Dear God ...

FABRE

What makes you so sure?

PHILIPPEAUX

Every time he opens his mouth Danton discredits the government. Robespierre won't allow that.

WESTERMANN

Robespierre, always bloody Robespierre. Not even a man – a lawyer!

DELACROIX

We're all lawyers.

DANTON

(Enters swiftly)

News, friends! Where the hell are the candles?

He lights candles.

HERAULT

Oh, my God, this place! To find oneself in a dog kennel!

DANTON

Never mind, friends. Never mind. What does it matter? Tomorrow we go home!

CAMILLE

Home? Oh, sweet Jesus –

FABRE

Do you mean it, Georges?

DANTON

Of course I mean it!

DELACROIX
Oh, stop it. Why don't you stop?

He moves away.

DANTON
Lucille has collected over five thousand livres.

CAMILLE
Lucille? Is she all right?

DANTON
Of course she's all right. Now, listen. Some of the Committee of General Security have taken bribes. Tomorrow, a squadron from the suburbs will surround the Tribunal building!

WESTERMANN whoops.

DANTON
We can count on three Communes already and, at noon – at noon, my friends – General Charbonnier will enter Paris with six thousand men!

WESTERMANN
Charbonnier – here?

HERAULT
Troops! Hurrah!

FABRE
Do you mean it, Georges?

DANTON
Of course I mean it! Friends, the whole of France is waiting out there to defend us! Once I'm on my feet tomorrow, they'll be forced to produce our witnesses. They'll have no choice! By the end of the day – my God – we'll be shoulder high, carried through the

ACT THREE

cheering crowds, as Robespierre slips down the steps
of the tumbril!

HERAULT

Georges, you're a man of genius.

DANTON

Trust me – trust me. And now, friends, sleep! We
have a long day ahead of us tomorrow. (*He lies back.*)
Ahh, that's better. (*He leans over to put out the
candle.*)

CAMILLE

No, don't! (*DANTON lies back, leaving the candle
alight.*) Impossible to sleep.

DANTON

Then dream of future pleasures.

CAMILLE

(*Drily*)

As a revolutionary?

DANTON

Why not? Is virtue only to be found in work – in pain?
Why not fine horses, fine women – music – a life of
splendour for all. Why not? We live to live, Camille.
(*Softly*) My God, what a heavenly country! Forests,
fields, rivers ... the pink snows of the Alps ... warm
beaches, wine, figs ... a handful of olives – Ohh,
La Belle France! And Paris! And I thought I'd had
enough. Blood, stench, I'd had my fill. But enough of
life? Never! I want it, here, now – all of it in my hands.
Christ, I can't wait for the light! I want my boots on!
Georges Danton, tired of life? Great God, I am life. I
could eat it. (*He lies back.*)

Silence. Suddenly, he sits up in a panic. He feels his neck, and gasps.

>PHILIPPEAUX
>*(Calls softly)*

Danton ...

DANTON freezes.

>DANTON

What do you want?

>PHILIPPEAUX

To speak to you?

>DANTON

I thought I was a thief and a scoundrel.

>PHILIPPEAUX

You are, but what's the difference? We're both standing by our graves.

>DANTON

Very well. (*Gets up and shakes hands.*) Treaty to be annulled, I take it, when we're freed tomorrow?

>PHILIPPEAUX
>*(Slight pause.)*

Do you think it's good to give these men false hopes?

>DANTON
>*(Shrugs.)*

I may have exaggerated the odds, but we have a chance.

>PHILIPPEAUX

On the contrary. By arousing the antagonism of the court, you have condemned every man here to death.

ACT THREE

DANTON

This gamble is not for pygmies. It's for France. The world! Can they make a revolution? Without a man of genius to haul them up? No. History, my friend, is created by the individual, not the masses.

PHILIPPEAUX

(Slight pause. Murmurs)

So, you would be our dictator?

DANTON

I have the capacity. And, sometimes, I have dreamed of my little Louise, a crown on her head, looking up at me in admiration. But you and I both know the realities, the impossibility of power.

PHILIPPEAUX

(Dejected)

Our great experiment has failed. The people can't see what we've tried to do for them.

DANTON

(Growls)

The further you push them towards virtue, the harder they'll kick you in the face.

PHILIPPEAUX

Why?

DANTON

How should I know?

PHILIPPEAUX

Perhaps we must make virtue more enticing. *(Slight pause.)* Danton, we are all capable of nobility. He asks it of us. *(He grasps DANTON's sleeve.)* Save the Revolution! Write to him publicly, this at least you –

DANTON

Save it? For him? You mean, concede?

PHILIPPEAUX

My dear Danton, you must know it's all over.

DANTON

Over?

PHILIPPEAUX

Yes. You're deluding yourself. We're already dead.

DANTON

What! Robespierre murder Danton? (*Laughs*) Watch me tomorrow. Does he think he can cut me down like a common conscript? I'll choke the life out of him!

PHILIPPEAUX

So, this is what the revolution has come to.

DANTON

I am the Revolution! You think it will survive me? The Terror's creeping up through the cobbles. It's spreading like weed on a pond. Can't you smell it? There's a reek, a stink in the air, from here to the Baltic! Robespierre wins? Robespierre – take the light from Danton? (*He utters a howl. His knees giving way*) All right. All right. All right, but he pays. You all pay! I'll take every one of you with me!

PHILIPPEAUX

Oh Danton. (*He turns to the wall.*)

DANTON

Philippeaux?

But there is no response.

Blackout.

ACT THREE

ACT THREE - SCENE SEVEN

The Committee of Public Safety.

CARNOT, BARERE, COLLOT, and SAINT-JUST are seated at table. ROBESPIERRE is on his feet.

>BARERE
>
>How can we refuse them witnesses? On what grounds?
>
>CARNOT
>
>I tell you it's illegal!
>
>COLLOT
>
>That letter was addressed to the Committee of Public Safety, not to you!
>
>CARNOT
>
>*(Banging the table)*
>
>Give it up, damn you!
>
>ROBESPIERRE
>
>*(Pauses for silence.)*
>
>Under no circumstances.
>
>COLLOT
>
>Do you want us all killed?

BILLAUD enters swiftly.

>BILLAUD
>
>Robespierre, is it true?
>
>ROBESPIERRE
>
>That I intercepted a letter? Yes.

BILLAUD

Thank God! (*He collapses on to a seat.*) Destroy it, please! I denied its existence. If you don't destroy it, I'm a dead man!

CARNOT

What do you mean?

BARERE

Why?

COLLOT AND BARERE

What's happened?

BILLAUD

(*Still breathless*)

Danton's star is rising by the minute! Keep away, Robespierre. They're ready to kill you. Our arrests are imminent!

SAINT-JUST dashes to the door.

BILLAUD

The galleries have gone mad. Fouquier can't hold them! Danton's friends are armed and everywhere! They're about to storm the building!

BARERE

It's over. We're finished.

BILLAUD

What's to be done?

BARERE

(*Small*)

Robespierre?

SAINT-JUST returns.

ACT THREE

> ROBESPIERRE

He must be removed from the trial.

> CARNOT

Danton?

> BARERE AND CARNOT

How?

> ROBESPIERRE

I don't know.

He sits suddenly, as though his strength has gone.

> ROBESPIERRE

For the moment, I cannot see a way forward. But we must not back down.

> BARERE

You heard! Our lives are threatened!

> CARNOT

We shall have to give in. I make a proposal that we instruct the court to release Danton at once.

> COLLOT

I second that!

> BARERE

Maxime, you said yourself – what do humiliations matter when the survival of the government is at stake?

ROBESPIERRE remains, head bowed, hands together.

> COLLOT
> *(Whispers, furious.)*

What's he doing? Praying?

CARNOT
As a matter of policy, it might be better if you remove yourself...

BILLAUD
The Committee might then survive.

ROBESPIERRE
(*Rises*)
Survive? With a government of cringing cowards? Saint-Just – go to the Jacobin Club. Bring every member of the Convention to the Tribunal. I shall go there now myself and demand a verdict.

BILLAUD
But it's your name they're yelling. They won't let you utter a word!

COLLOT
Let him risk his own life! What's happened...

VADIER enters, out of breath.

VADIER
We're...(*Gasps*)...we're surrounded.... the whole of Paris...

SAINT-JUST
Bluff!

VADIER
They've had agents in the prison...

ROBESPIERRE
I knew it!

VADIER
One of the prisoners, Laflotte, ex-envoy to Venice, corroborates everything. Desmoulins' wife has been

ACT THREE

all over Paris, bribing on a huge scale. They mean
to open up the prisons and storm the Tuileries ...
uhhh ...

Silence but for the rasping of his breath.

BARERE

Well?

COLLOT

Well, Robespierre?

CARNOT

What now?

ROBESPIERRE

What now? What now? I will tell you. Your miserable
lives have been saved.

Reaction.

ROBESPIERRE

This conspiracy gives us the weapon that we need.
By surrounding the Tribunal, Danton threatens
the Convention. Every member must now support
whatever emergency measures we see fit to impose.
(To BILLAUD) Order troops to surround the building.

BILLAUD

Very well.

SAINT-JUST

Splendid!

Murmurs of support.

ROBESPIERRE

You do – all of you – realise what this means?

Silence. They gaze at him.

ROBESPIERRE

It means this government steps irrevocably on to the path of Terror.

SAINT-JUST

Mind what you say.

ROBESPIERRE

(Turns on him ferociously)

You too, my friend. You too should know what you are doing and where it will take you. We must slaughter the fools who have concocted this farce. Their massacre will cause outrage and more conspiracy. We shall have to kill, kill, kill. All day long. Executioners of the people on behalf of the people. Thus, we regress and our ideals perish.

BARERE

Why?

ROBESPIERRE

(Tired.)

Because in order to survive this day, and those to come, we must concentrate power in our own hands.

CARNOT

(Softly)

Dictatorship, Robespierre?

COLLOT

You bloody Judas!

SAINT-JUST

(Jumps on a chair)

Don't you understand what he's trying to say? The dilemma we face ...!

ACT THREE

ROBESPIERRE
(Soft)

Antoine ...

SAINT-JUST

What? *(Climbs down.)* What?

ROBESPIERRE

It is a valid point. If I have overstepped my function then that is an error to be corrected.

BARERE

Maxime, that's hardly necessary.

ROBESPIERRE

I submit myself to you. Appoint a commission. Go through my speeches ...

SAINT-JUST
(Quickly)

I applaud our colleague's open and willing readiness to ...

ROBESPIERRE

No. I mean it. Billaud. Carnot. Saint-Just ... you are as capable as I. If I have done harm to this revolution – to my country – then I ask you, humbly, to redress it. And to condemn me.

BILLAUD

Don't be in such a hurry for the guillotine, Citizen. In any case, this is not the moment. There is a battle to be won ...

VADIER

We're wasting time. (*To ROBESPIERRE*) Are you prepared to come down to the floor of the Tribunal and denounce this conspiracy?

They wait.

> ROBESPIERRE
> *(Collapses in his chair.)*
> I'm sorry. I can't. My voice has gone. As you know, I've been ill.

> SAINT-JUST
> I'll go.

> ROBESPIERRE
> Perhaps you should all go together.

> BARERE
> You think so? Must we? Should we?

> BILLAUD
> We'll go together.

> CARNOT
> Very well. *(Leads the way.)*

> ROBESPIERRE
> Gentlemen ...

They turn.

> ROBESPIERRE
> The fact that the Dantonistes are demanding witnesses is not even worth mentioning. Please remember that.

They look at one another but, under his scrutiny, they go.

ROBESPIERRE remains at the table, stiff and formal. His eyes closed.

END OF ACT THREE

ACT FOUR

ACT FOUR - SCENE ONE

The Tribunal.

HERMANN, plus TWO OTHER JUDGES, sit at a desk on a raised platform. Seated in the Dock are DANTON, CAMILLE, DELACROIX, FABRE, HERAULT, PHILIPPEAUX and WESTERMANN.

FOUQUIER is on his feet, his hoarse voice imitated constantly by the PEOPLE in the galleries.

> FOUQUIER
> Sit down, Danton. You have no right to speak!

> DANTON
> Take it away from me then! He thinks he's got our
> heads in the basket already! Made you a promise,
> have they, that you'll keep yours?

Cheers and laughter.

> FOUQUIER
> He calls himself ... he calls himself the Man of the
> Tenth of August! We know where he was that night.
> At home! While the rest of us risked our lives!

> DANTON
> Slander!

> FOUQUIER
> Sat by his own fireside while our blood ran in the
> streets! I was there!

DANTON

And where was Citizen Robespierre? In the cellar! Buried up to his balls in coal!

Laughter.

FOUQUIER
(Shaking his head)
Some of us know the facts!

DANTON

The facts? Oh, don't be in a hurry to hear those, old friend – you might regret it! We can all come with a few facts!

WOMAN 1

Let them have it, Georges! Bring them down!

WOMAN 2

Danton! Danton! *(The chant is taken up.)*

FOUQUIER
(Bangs table furiously.)
We've lost three days ... *(Noise)* Three days you've had to answer the charges against you! If you've nothing more to say – sit down!

Shouts and hissing.

FOUQUIER
(He bawls.)
Do any of the accused wish to add to their defence?

Consternation among the accused. They shout out.

DANTON
(Shouts.)
This hearing will be over when I say it's over!

ACT FOUR

The Jury, baffled, rise, and sit down again.

DANTON

Countrymen! I have been your comrade and leader for five long years!

Applause throughout his speech.

DANTON

Liberty itself shines on this face! Look at it! With you, this face threw down the rotten throne and kicked the crowns from their stinking heads! Citizens! Were you there? Does this face lie? Was it Georges Danton who led you? Was it his voice you heard?

A deafening response, ending in sporadic shouts.

WOMAN 3

We remember!

MAN 1

We haven't forgotten, Danton!

MAN 2

(Loud voice)

And we haven't forgotten the money that somehow got lost from the Treasury, Georges!

Laughter.

DANTON

That's it. That's the sort of lie they're peddling! Let's obscure his merits. How many lies can we spread? Envy, friends, envy! Citizens of France, I appeal to you! Are we, or are we not, entitled to call witnesses in our defence?!!

A roar of affirmation.

FOUQUIER
The defendant is forbidden to provoke the public!

DANTON
Where are they?

The chant is taken up. "Where are they? Where are they!"

DANTON
(Bawls above them.)
We will answer the charges against us when our witnesses are produced and heard, and only then do you have the right to close proceedings!

HERMANN
Since the Convention initiated the charges, its members cannot be called for the defence!

As the chants for witnesses become louder.

DANTON
Do you hear that, people of France? I appeal to you from this parody of a court! You and only you have the right to try me!

Uproar.

FOUQUIER
Clear the court! Clear the court! Clear the court! The court will be cleared while the jury retires. The jury will retire now!

DANTON
Friends, your turn will be next! This is an attempt at murder. Murder, friends! Murder!!!

The sign for DANTON'S SUPPORTERS to go on the offensive.

ACT FOUR

DANTON'S SUPPORTERS

Traitors! Where are the witnesses? Murder! Acquittal! Acquittal!

The sounds modulate for shouts of 'Danton!' and 'Long Live Danton!'

CAMILLE

People of France, we are being murdered!

DANTON

Courage, brothers! Force against force!

WESTERMANN

(Leaps on to the table.)

Together we stormed the Bastille! Together we stormed the Tuileries! Attack! Together! Now!

There is a rush forward and DANTON is lifted shoulder-high.

SOLDIERS run in. Three shots ring out. PEOPLE crouch at once. Silence. Then DANTON rises.

DANTON

Now you see, friends, now you see! *(To a YOUNG SOLDIER)* What are you going to do? Cut out my tongue with a bayonet?

The SOLDIERS push the crowd back.

DANTON

People of France!

FOUQUIER

If you persist I shall have you removed.

MAN 1

Shut up! Danton! Don't play their game!

MAN 2
Rogues and embezzlers, the lot of them – and you, Georges!

Some laughter. DANTON waits for silence.

DANTON
Very well. As you wish. So far, I've been silent.

A loud guffaw.

DANTON
Now – I accuse. Do you know why – why they have laid their hands on my life? Because I, Georges Danton, am the only barrier between Maximilian Robespierre and his ascent to the throne of France!

Reaction.

FOUQUIER
That's enough! That slander alone has sealed your fate, my friend!

But the galleries shout for DANTON, and FOUQUIER gives way.

DANTON
For five long years Robespierre has crept towards the crown. I, and I alone, have seen his intention. Friends! You see before you the revolutionary troops turned against the people of France! Who has done this? Robespierre. Maxime Robespierre!

VOICES
Down with Robespierre! Down with Robespierre!

HERMANN
All stand for the representatives of the people!

The Committee of Public Safety enter – including BILLAUD, COLLOT, BARERE, CARNOT, VADIER and SAINT-JUST.

ACT FOUR

BILLAUD

Citizens! Citizens! A conspiracy has been discovered against the lawful government of this nation! The wife of the accused, Camille Desmoulins, has incited an uprising ...

CAMILLE

Lucille! Lucille!

BILLAUD

... against the people of France! Enemy agents are among you!

DANTON

(Shouts above the noise.)

Lies! Lies! Lies!

The SUPPORTERS panic. The accused turn on DANTON.

DELACROIX

(To DANTON)

You've sent us to our graves, damn you!

FOUQUIER

(Shouts)

Be quiet! Silence! Silence! *(As order is restored.)* The names of all present will be taken ...and listed.

Achieving total silence by this threat, he nods to HERMANN to continue.

HERMANN

(Reads document.)

The National Convention decrees the following: that the Revolutionary Tribunal shall bring proceedings in the Danton Affair to a close without further adjournment. Defendants who resist the authority of this court or who behave in a derogatory manner ...

DANTON
Citizens, you are my witnesses! Have we resisted?
Have we behaved in a derogatory manner?

MAN 3 YOUNG VOICE
No! *(Murmurs of agreement. But louder jeers.)*

MAN 2
Only now and then, Georges!

Laughter.

DELACROIX
(To DANTON)
Congratulations.

HERMANN
Members of the jury, how do you find?

JURY FOREMAN
(Rises, nervous. Speaks in a small voice.)

Guilty.

He sits.

HERMANN
Sentence to be passed in one hour. Clear the Court.

Silence. The accused are aghast. WESTERMANN clenches his fist, mutters, curses. CAMILLE's eyes roll.

FABRE
My God – it's over!

DANTON rises, eyes wide. He staggers, recovers himself.

DANTON
People of France. I stand before you ...to offer a gift.
To offer you myself. My love. Everything. You are
my mission, my cause, my reason for living. Look at

this right arm – it's yours! You own it. You've had my body, mind and soul, twenty hours a day – and you see me still on my feet! Can this be done by the weak, the small, the spiteful?

Shouts of 'No!'

DANTON

My people, haven't you suffered enough? Isn't it time we ate again, drank again – sat by warm fires again? What kind of revolution are we creating? An arid state, to reduce us to names on a list? Laws created not to enrich life, but to threaten and subdue! Make no mistake, it is you – and only you – who have the right to choose who shall lead us into the nineteenth century, to a bright, joyous, delicious life – or to a misery such as you have not, my friends, yet dreamed of. Those who repress you in your name are liars and traitors. Not only to this country, but to life itself! Look at me. Stand with me. Together, and only together, can we defeat the forces of oppression. What have I ever asked but to be allowed to struggle for you, and haul you up into the light beside me? Am I not yours? I – Danton – your servant. Your slave! Look into my eyes...into the eyes of Danton! Friends... Have I ever failed you?

MAN 1

No!!

Murmurs of agreement.

DANTON

Have I ever sold you short?

Silence, then a solitary snicker.

                    MAN 2

You've done all right for yourself, Georges!

                    WOMAN 1

He's done well enough!

                    WOMAN 2

Look at his belly!

                    MAN 3

Bought himself a pretty young wife!

                    MAN 4

What happened to the army funds, Georges?

                    WOMAN 1

Look at his coat!

                    MAN 1

Danton, the Dandy!

                    WOMAN 2

Come on, Georges, give us a smile!

                    MAN 2

He'll be smiling tomorrow!

Laughter, and then silence. DANTON glares. He looks about him, his manner calm, almost gentle.

                    DANTON

You vile, stinking rubbish. What are you, you braying gobs of offal? Laugh, would you? When you should be pissing yourselves in shame! Oh, you'll roar like lions when some weakling is crushed underfoot but – courage? Loyalty?

                    CAMILLE
                    (Shrieks)

Judases!!

ACT FOUR

DANTON

(Turns briefly.)

Judases? *(Turns back to the crowd.)* You? Don't even aspire. You? The people? Take over the world? Allow me to make room for you. My light...my air...my breath...all yours! A last and temporary gift as I abandon you.

WOMAN 4

(Lone wail)

Oh Georges...!

DANTON

(Bows, ironic.)

My felicitations. I leave you to the jaws of a tiger. You'll be up to your eyeballs in blood. Can't you hear its wheels creaking? The cart? For you, and you, and you!

They flinch away from him.

DANTON

And for him! For Robespierre! Rotting in his shroud. Rotting, dissolving, beside the bones of the patriot – Georges Danton!!

Silence.

FOUQUIER

(Banal)

Have you finished?

DANTON turns on him so violently that he winces, even at a distance.

DANTON

(To the Jury.)

As for you, you hang-dogs...you're lower than rat-shit.

                    FOUQUIER

    Take him down.

DANTON laughs loudly. Jumps down, and strides ahead of the TWO SOLDIERS. CAMILLE jumps to his feet, tears up his documents, and throws them in HERMANN's face.

                    CAMILLE

    Murderers. Murderers!

TWO SOLDIERS grasp him. He breaks free.

                    CAMILLE

    Let me go, damn you! I won't be butchered like a calf!

The Galleries laugh.

                    CAMILLE

    I want to defend myself. I'm innocent. I want to speak
    to the judges.

He is dragged away.

                    CAMILLE

    You swine! You animals! You're not human! Don't!
    No ...no!

Laughter and clapping.

                    FABRE
                (Rises with difficulty.)
    The honourable Tribunal will allow me to excuse
    myself. I trust that you've enjoyed the comedy.

He bows, and limps out, to applause. DELACROIX rises, shocked, and leaves. HERAULT follows, turns.

                    HERAULT
                (Frightened.)
    Long live the Revolution!

ACT FOUR

WOMAN

Oh, he's too young!

She is immediately arrested.

PHILIPPEAUX bows and leaves, to jeers.

WESTERMANN

Seven wounds. Seven wounds I've taken for France. And all in front – none behind. And that's my accusation to you! Kiss me goodbye, you rabble, you know where!

He bares his backside to the crowd, who burst into cheers and whistles.

FOUQUIER

Clear the court! Clear the court!

The SOLDIERS clear the court. HERMANN joins FOUQUIER, wiping his face.

HERMANN

Thank God, it's over!

FOUQUIER

I've got a headache.

HERMANN

Monsieur Fouquier?

FOUQUIER

(Snarls.)

I've got a bloody headache!

HERMANN

The jury will vote it? The verdict?

FOUQUIER

(Evilly)

Oh, they'll vote it all right. I've seen to that. Oh yes, we gaffed that salmon all right.

He lets out a huge groan.

HERMANN

What is it?

FOUQUIER

(Turns on him)

You think it's going to be easy? With Robespierre?

HERMANN stammers, frightened.

FOUQUIER

(He imitates Robespierre's voice)

"You will deprive him of his right to speak!" Easy enough to say! Work for Robespierre? *(Turns and, on his way out)* Jesus Christ!

HERMANN, following, gives his back a wry look.

Fade out.

ACT FOUR - SCENE TWO

A vaulted basement in the Conciergerie.

Narrow staircase to ground level, as in the painting by Muller. SOLDIERS on guard. SANSON, the executioner – a modest, dapper man – with TWO ASSISTANTS and FOUR BARBERS listen to DANTON who is offstage.

ACT FOUR

CLERK

(Offstage)

... and accomplices, guilty of both conspiracies ...

DANTON

(Offstage)

Murderers!

CLERK

(Offstage. Voice unclear)

... against the safety of the Republic ...

DANTON

(Offstage)

Republic? You snivelling cowards! What Republic? Whose Republic?

Crowd noise.

CLERK

(Offstage)

... to death by beheading ...

DANTON

(Offstage)

Rabble! Rabble! We'll see who is the judge! Leave it to History ... to History ...!

He rushes in, sees those present, reacts, ending his tirade ironically.

DANTON

... to History.

BARBER indicates chair.

DANTON

Ah yes.

DANTON tears off his collar.

> DANTON
> *(Over his shoulder)*
>
> Get on with it.

The BARBER starts to cut his hair.

TWO SOLDIERS bring in DELACROIX, tense, WESTERMANN, black with rage, and PHILIPPEAUX. They sit. Silence, except for the sound of the scissors.

> DANTON
> *(Quietly)*
>
> I'm leaving the chaos behind me. Not one of them knows how to govern. It'll be the sick and shit of Terror from now on. Ho ho ho! The heads will roll! There won't be a head of hair left in Paris.

> BARBER
>
> Please Citizen, I may cut you ...

> DANTON
> *(Indicating SANSON)*
>
> Taking the bread out of that gentleman's mouth, eh?

SANSON lowers his eyes discreetly.

> DANTON
> *(Calls.)*
>
> Don't forget! Thick neck! Remember Louis. Don't take two goes at it!

The BARBER snips.

> DANTON
>
> Everything – the whole of the Revolution is my work. I've carried France on my shoulders.

ACT FOUR

> PHILIPPEAUX
>
> That's enough, Danton. You can't shout away the fear.
> I've tried. It's better not to.
>
> DANTON
>
> It's this country I tremble for. An hour before he gave
> the order for Camille's arrest, he was cooing tender
> friendship – the sodomist!

DANTON shakes his head.

> BARBER
>
> Sir, please don't move your head.
>
> DANTON
>
> *(Snorts)*
>
> All right, so he's got what he wants. Three months.
> That's what I give him. Three months before he's
> worms.

They are interrupted by the entrance of FOUR SOLDIERS and FABRE, HERAULT and CAMILLE. Dazed, CAMILLE sways.

> FABRE
>
> What now? Oh, I see.

FABRE, HERAULT and CAMILLE are seated to have their collars removed and their hair cut.

> PHILIPPEAUX
>
> Yes, Robespierre will fall.

DANTON rises. CAMILLE gives a piercing shriek as the scissors touch his neck.

> FABRE
>
> Stop it, damn you!

ASSISTANT #1 approaches PHILIPPEAUX with a short length of rope. PHLIPPEAUX puts his hands behind his back to be tied. ASSISTANT #2 approaches DANTON, with rope.

> DANTON
> *(Breaks down. Low.)*

Please, in a moment.

He collapses on to a chair.

> DANTON
> *(Murmurs.)*

I feel sick.

> WESTERMANN
> *(Cruel)*

Poor Georges!

ASSISTANT #2 ties DANTON's hands behind his back. After tying PHILIPPEAUX's hands, ASSISTANT #1 and SOLDIERS #1, #2, #3 and #4 tie the hands of DELACROIX, CAMILLE, HERAULT, FABRE and WESTERMANN.

> CAMILLE
> *(Simply)*

You stole my talents. You didn't even use them. Because of you Lucille will die. You've stolen my life – tricked me out of it. Why? What good has it done you?

> WESTERMANN

To throw it all away by listening to a civilian!

> DANTON

Go on, you blundering whiners. You took your chance, the same as me. D'you think I regret one minute of it? You fools! I've lived! I've had a life! Tell me something I haven't had – haven't enjoyed! I've had everything!

ACT FOUR

I'm full. Full up! Can Robespierre say as much when his head falls in the basket?

DELACROIX
Keep up the lies, Danton!

SANSON
Are you ready, gentlemen?

CAMILLE collapses.

At a wave from SANSON, SOLDIER #1 helps him to his feet.

DANTON looks sympathetically at CAMILLE, then straightens up.

DANTON
Forward, brothers! Be proud! Be proud of what we have accomplished! Our names will shine in the annals of History!

DELACROIX
(Smiles ruefully)
Bravo Georges! France is losing a great actor.

DANTON begins to sing 'La Marseillaise.' All sing as they march off – the SOLDIERS falling in behind, followed by SANSON.

Light change.

ACT FOUR – SCENE THREE

Robespierre's Salon.

ROBESPIERRE is alone, reclining on a day bed.

The SOUND of the carts, and the singing of the Marseillaise.

CAMILLE
(Offstage)
Maxime, Maxime! They're killing me! Maxime!

DANTON
(Offstage)
I leave you my testicles, Robespierre! You'll need them!

The SOUNDS begin to fade.

ELEONORE, white-faced, glides in noiselessly.

ELEONORE
(Softly)
The evening post, Maxime ...

ROBESPIERRE
(Unnaturally loud)
Thank you.

ELEONORE slips away. The sounds die to an eerie silence.

SAINT-JUST's characteristic knock.

ROBESPIERRE
(After a sizeable pause)
Come in. Any sign of trouble?

SAINT-JUST
No, the crowd are in a good mood. They were laughing at Camille.

ROBESPIERRE
I heard them. (*SAINT-JUST drums his fingers.*) As you see, no need for alarm. Just another show for the mob.

ACT FOUR

SAINT-JUST

That same mob captured the Bastille. And broke into the Tuileries without taking so much as a spoon.

ROBESPIERRE

(Sits up.)

You are right. I stand corrected.

SAINT-JUST

You know what you have to do now, don't you?

ROBESPIERRE

Not now, Antoine, I'm tired.

SAINT-JUST

Assume the dictatorship.

ROBESPIERRE

Oh, stop nagging me. *(He rises, paces. Turns to SAINT-JUST.)* Tell me something. If there is to be a dictator, why me? Why not you?

SAINT-JUST

Because you're a man of genius.

ROBESPIERRE

You don't consider yourself my equal?

SAINT-JUST

No! We've seen what happens. A chance of preferment and even the purest revolutionary goes bad. But not you. You're incorruptible. *(He stands over him with grim fondness.)* You're ill.

ROBESPIERRE

No, not ill. Lost.

SAINT-JUST

Lost? You know precisely what must be done.

ROBESPIERRE
I know nothing.

SAINT-JUST
Maxime, you are responsible for the lives and futures of twenty-five million people. Without you, the revolution will cease to exist. It doesn't matter whether you wish to assume power or not. You have to, or everything is lost.

ROBESPIERRE
(Groans aloud.)
One thought! That was enough.

SAINT-JUST
Thought?

ROBESPIERRE
Could we be wrong?

SAINT-JUST
Maxime – you're tired. You said so yourself...

ROBESPIERRE
For the sake of the Republic, do you think I should step aside?

SAINT-JUST
No, of course not.

ROBESPIERRE
So, I should go on – in the dark. *(SAINT-JUST looks at him irritably.)* You truly believe a dictatorship is necessary?

SAINT-JUST
No doubt about it.

ACT FOUR

ROBESPIERRE

You think the people don't have the ability, or the desire, to govern themselves?

SAINT-JUST

Do you?

ROBESPIERRE

So, you're saying that the foundation of our new system – that democracy – is an illusion.

SAINT-JUST

This is a crisis, Maxime. We need urgent measures!

He crosses and puts a hand on ROBESPIERRE's shoulder.

SAINT-JUST

Democracy – autocracy – what does it matter? Do you think people care what sort of government they have so long as it gives them decent lives?

ROBESPIERRE

So, freedom and democracy are an illusion.

SAINT-JUST

They're what's kept this Revolution alive! If they are illusions . . .

ROBESPIERRE looks at him doubtfully.

SAINT-JUST

. . . we need them. They're worth dying for.

ROBESPIERRE

Worth dying? For a lie?

His legs give way and he collapses into a chair.

Pause.

ROBESPIERRE

Perhaps I'm going mad. (*He looks up.*) Is it madness, d'you think?

SAINT-JUST
(Surveys him)

No. You're tired.

Silence. ROBESPIERRE lies back, sighs, relaxing, and moves gently, making himself comfortable.

ROBESPIERRE

Antoine ...

SAINT-JUST

Yes?

ROBESPIERRE

Don't wake me as you leave. I'm falling asleep.

SAINT-JUST nods then BARERE enters – evades SAINT-JUST – and approaches ROBESPIERRE urgently.

BARERE

I'm sorry. May I ...?

ROBESPIERRE
(Giving him a deadly look)

You already have.

BARERE

I'm awfully sorry but we need your advice.

ROBESPIERRE

I'm afraid that, for once, you will have to do without me.

SAINT-JUST

Can't it wait until tomorrow?

ACT FOUR

> BARERE
>
> Impossible.
>
> ROBESPIERRE
>
> *(Waves SAINT-JUST away)*
>
> Very well, what is it?
>
> BARERE
>
> The prison conspiracy.

ROBESPIERRE is at once alert.

> BARERE
>
> Some of us feel the matter should be treated lightly, as you implied. We're prepared to settle for a few examples. Madame Desmoulins ...
>
> ROBESPIERRE
>
> If the need is felt.
>
> BARERE
>
> But the Committee of General Security want severe reprisals!

ROBESPIERRE rises.

> BARERE
>
> You'll come? We've adjourned for half an hour.
>
> ROBESPIERRE
>
> Of course.
>
> BARERE
>
> I'll tell them.

BARERE goes. ROBESPIERRE begins pacing.

> ROBESPIERRE
>
> I need two years to reconstruct this government! Two years! Perhaps, if we give them all enough

to do, there'll be no time for factions. (*Paces.*)
The Committee must command respect! The
revolutionary spirit must be revived. Purified. Both
here and in the country. Oh, and there's no time!

SAINT-JUST

No time? What do you mean? You're still young!

ROBESPIERRE

Corruption. Corruption keeps hauling us down. It
hangs over me ... dogs me – like Danton. Everywhere
I turn I feel its breath on my skull. (*Turns to face
SAINT-JUST.*) How do we protect ourselves from the
cannibals?

He is overcome by a fearsome bout of coughing.

He gasps. Recovering, at last, he smiles grimly.

ROBESPIERRE

And now a decline into consumption, it seems.

SAINT-JUST

No ...

ROBESPIERRE

No. (*Waves his hand.*) Perhaps not.

SOUND of PEOPLE and CARTS.

ROBESPIERRE

Listen! They're coming back.

They listen.

SAINT-JUST

It's over. No more Danton.

ROBESPIERRE

I hope you're right.

ACT FOUR

The noise of the people and carts swells and dies away.

SAINT-JUST

Your sleeve's caught.

ROBESPIERRE

Oh.

ROBESPIERRE carefully puts his coat to rights.

ROBESPIERRE

You know, Antoine ... if I truly believed that life had no meaning. That nothing mattered. I think I could bear it. Even be happy. *(Glances at him.)* Does that shock you?

SAINT-JUST

Nothing shocks me anymore.

ROBESPIERRE

(Looks at his watch.)

Time to go.

Blackout.

The End.

THE INCORRUPTIBLE

Cast breakdown

1. Maximilian Robespierre
2. Georges-Jacques Danton
3. Camille Desmoulins
4. Antoine Saint-Just
5. General Westermann
6. Delacroix – Freron
7. Eleonore Duplay – Citizen #3 – Woman #1
8. Louise Danton – Woman #2
9. Philippeaux – Soldier #1– Citizen #2
10. Lucille Desmoulins – Woman #3
11. Bourdon – Tribunal Usher – Jury Foreman – Sanson
12. Vadier – Chaumette – Fouquier-Tinville
13. Collot d'Herbois – Merlin – Comte D'Estaing
14. Billaud-Varenne – Judge #1 – Barber #3
15. Lindet – Lecointre – Hermann
16. Carnot – Convention Secretary – Tallien – Judge #2 – Assistant #2
17. Barère – Legendre – Fabre d'Eglantine – Barber #4
18. Courtois – Clerk
19. Barber – Laflotte – Citizen #1 – Man #4 – Barber #1
20. Messenger – Robespierre's Secretary – Legrand – Soldier #3 – Usher #2 – Man #2 – Assistant #1
21. Waiter – Soldier #2 – Panis – Le Vicomte D'Estaing
22. Danton's Secretary – Young Officer – Usher #1 – Herault
23. ASM #1 Guard – Man #1 – Barber #2
24. ASM #2 Woman #4 – Citizen

Can be performed with 19 men, 3 women and 2 ASMs

GARIBALDI, SI!

Giuseppe Garibaldi

For Alfred Molina

FOREWORD

Garibaldi, in his day, was an international star. During his lifetime, photography began to be used commercially, so that his face became familiar in Europe and beyond. He was handsome – which helped – a northern Italian, fair with a straight nose and a steady gaze. Not tall.

The gaze was that of a seaman. Giuseppe Garibaldi came from the port of Nice – Nizza as it was then under the rule of Savoy. He went to sea early, wisely taking ship after being implicated in the Young Italy movement.

This early involvement in the creation of one Italy from small states dominated by outside powers was prophetic. The notion of the nation state was emerging from the medievalism of empires encompassing peoples of different languages, customs and creeds.

From the American War of Independence and the French Revolution had sprung ideas of freedom, of democratic self-government.

Garibaldi became a guerrilla fighter in South America. He was anti-religious and anti-royal – although he made an exception for Queen Victoria. ("She's a fine little woman, so as far as I'm concerned she's a Republican.") In South America, he became a seasoned campaigner and tactician. He then returned to Italy and led the glorious Thousand from Sicily to Rome. The unification of Italy was achieved.

As the beloved hero of the Risorgimento, Garibaldi could have become King of Italy. Instead he retired to a rocky island – Caprera – off the coast of Tuscany.

Why is Garibaldi such a wonderful man? He was brave, wily, ferocious, but also soft-hearted. He said to his men before battle or a skirmish: "I absolutely forbid you to get killed." He was blood-thirsty when necessary. He had his own men shot for looting. He was gallant towards women. An audacious, resourceful man, capable of idiocy; a man of heart; a mixture of Ulysses and Hercules.

Today we would call him committed. Committed to the cause of an independent Italy he certainly was. What was unique was his rejection of place or prize. As an atheist, he expected no reward in heaven. What he respected was what was fair and decent. Above all, he understood the solution to heaven on earth – a life of simplicity.

Pam Gems

GARIBALDI, SI!

CHARACTERS

WILLIAM CAMPION
SPY
SIGNOR B.
FRANCESCA
GARIBALDI
SOLDIER #1
SOLDIER #2
SOLDIER #3
SOLDIER #4
BOY SOLDIER
SEAMSTRESS
CAPTAIN NINO BIXIO
ARTIST
GENERAL FRANCESCO CRISPI
CAPTAIN BARBONE
BOY RECRUIT
YOUNG MAN (VALERI)
KING VICTOR EMMANUEL II
PRINCE METTERNICH
COUNT CAVOUR
CAPTAIN ASTI
THE MARQUESA
SOLDIER #5
ENGLISH PROFESSOR
WOMAN IN NAPLES #1
WOMAN IN NAPLES #2
WOMAN IN NAPLES #3
BOY IN NAPLES

MAZZINI
MAYOR
CARDINAL
JESSIE
FRENCH GENERAL
AGNES
MR ATTRILL
GARDENER'S BOY
LADY TENNYSON
ALFRED, LORD TENNYSON
SOLDIER #6
SOLDIER #7

Can be performed with nine men, three women, one boy, two ASMs, and a horse.

GARIBALDI, SI!

ACT ONE

ACT ONE – SCENE ONE

Before curtain up, Verdi music, becoming more and more stirring. Crescendo as the curtain rises – topped by the very loud sound of cannon. Smoke, and the sounds of battle. Men running, crouched low.

> GARIBALDI
> *(Off stage)*
> Forward. Forward boys!

GARIBALDI enters on a white horse.

> GARIBALDI
> I absolutely forbid any man to get killed!

He yells – jumps down off the horse – and exits with sword and pistol. Noise – shouts – cries of the wounded. Cheers, prolonged. MUSIC tops this, then dies away to silence – except for birdsong.

Light change.

ACT ONE – SCENE TWO

The Island of Caprera.

As the smoke clears, we are in a rocky space with rocks for seats and flat rocks as tables. A view of the sea. Stage right a thicket, with a flat rock protruding. WILLIAM CAMPION, in neat travelling clothes, enters, followed by a MAN in a poncho (the SPY) who is carrying Campion's bag.

> CAMPION
> *(Looks around)*
> Are you sure this is the place?

> SPY
> Si, signor. The General! *(Points)*

> CAMPION
> *(Surprised)*
> Here?!

> SPY
> *(Proudly)*
> Si!

CAMPION looks at him doubtfully, but pays him. The SPY hides in the thicket, close by. An ELDERLY MAN, SIGNOR B, enters and nods amiably to CAMPION.

> SIGNOR B
> Good day, Signor.

> CAMPION
> Oh – good day to you.

> SIGNOR B
> Fine spot, eh? Caprera, you know, is an island.

> CAMPION
> Yes.

> SIGNOR B
> Surrounded by water, as indeed are all islands. Warm day, eh?

ACT ONE

CAMPION

Yes.

SIGNOR B

It's the weather.

He nods amiably and goes. CAMPION looks around, is startled by the sudden sound of a scolding female voice, fierce and screeching.

GARIBALDI enters abruptly. CAMPION moves forward, extending his hand.

CAMPION

General ...

GARIBALDI

Who are you? What do you want? *(Grabs him.)*

CAMPION

General, it is I, your English friend, William
Campion ... from The Times. You invited me
here – ow!

GARIBALDI

Speak up! Oh – it's you, what are you doing here?
You're the – *(searches his memory)* – the writer.

CAMPION straightens his clothes.

GARIBALDI

What was your name again?

CAMPION

William Campion. We met first in Sicily. I came out in
a bumboat to interview you.

GARIBALDI

That was a long time ago. *(Recognises him.)*
Campione – my friend – Campione!

He enfolds CAMPION in a warm embrace.

>GARIBALDI
>
>Sit down – sit down – make yourself comfortable.

CAMPION looks round. There are no chairs so he perches on a rock.

>GARIBALDI
>
>*(Calls)*
>
>Francesca! Francesca! *(Then, more subdued, gets up.)* I'll ...ah ...

FRANCESCA – a peasant woman, her sleeves rolled up – emerges, slams down a tray with a pitcher of wine and three glasses. She glares at them, and exits. GARIBALDI pours three large glasses of wine, limps over to the flat stone, places a glass of wine on it, and returns. CAMPION looks at the wine on the stone, and watches as a hand comes out of the bushes and takes the wine.

He looks at GARIBALDI.

>GARIBALDI
>
>Oh, that's just the spy.

>CAMPION
>
>The spy?

The SPY emerges briefly, doffs his cap and retires.

>GARIBALDI
>
>*(Pours wine for CAMPION and himself)*
>
>They send them over to keep an eye on me. Your health.

They drink. The SPY drains his glass, replaces it on the flat stone.

>CAMPION
>
>Hardly surprising, I suppose, General. You could have been the King of Italy if you'd wished.

ACT ONE

GARIBALDI

I could! I still could. I am a man of the people – the leader of the Thousand ...

GARIBALDI refills the SPY's glass.

GARIBALDI

...the conqueror of Naples, the creator of Italy. (*Pours wine.*) Not a bad chap. Makes himself useful bringing up the water, chopping wood. I help him with his reports. Can't write his own name.

They laugh.

CAMPION

And the other gentleman – with the beard?

GARIBALDI

Signor B. Joined us in Sicily. Not without courage but a bore. Unfortunately, by the time we found out it was too late to shoot him.

CAMPION

He's a lucky man. When we first met, General, you nearly had me killed.

GARIBALDI

I did! I remember!

A stream of Italian invective from FRANCESCA offstage.

GARIBALDI rises apologetically, and exits.

CAMPION waits.

Fado to black.

ACT ONE – SCENE THREE

An Army Encampment.

TWO SOLDIERS smoking in the sun. Another SOLDIER washing his shirt. A FOURTH SOLDIER washes himself out of a small bowl, and then drinks some of the water. FRANCESCA tends a cauldron.

A SEAMSTRESS darning the britches of a FIFTH SOLDIER, who is bending over for her to do it. CAMPION, in a velvet hat, with camera equipment, is waiting to interview GARIBALDI. With him is CAPTAIN BIXIO, raffish and handsome.

                    CAMPION
Is he a difficult man, Captain?

                    BIXIO
The General? God help you, no sir. Difficult? No. No, I wouldn't say difficult. In what way, difficult?

                    CAMPION
Oh, nothing really. It's just useful to know. As a journalist, you meet all sorts ... politicians, nobility, your artist. I always try for a little background material.

                    BIXIO
He's a brave man, sir.

                    CAMPION
Oh, no question of that! And you've been with him since ...

                    BIXIO
Since Austria, sir. Glorious days. Cutting our way through the hills, living on blackberries and goat's cheese. Of course, he never eats anything.

ACT ONE

CAMPION
(Grabbing for his notebook)
I beg your pardon?

BIXIO
The General. Doesn't eat. Just bread and apples.

CAMPION
Good Lord. Does he drink?

BIXIO
Not a lot. He watches his temper.

CAMPION
Ah, yes. Are there any ... areas to avoid?

BIXIO
No, he'll go anywhere.

CAMPION
What? Oh ... yes.

Pause.

The TWO SOLDIERS start to fight all over the place, until SOLDIER #1 sticks a dagger into SOLDIER #2 – who collapses and moans. His 'enemy' takes the bucket of suds from SOLDIER #3 who has been washing and scrubbing his shirt, and sluices down his mate's chest wound. He tears up SOLDIER 3's shirt. Whereupon SOLDIER #3 leaps upon him, and there is another fight. CAMPION is knocked over.

The TWO SOLDIERS fight their way offstage, leaving the wounded MAN moaning piteously.

CAMPION
Captain! That man's received a wound! A knife-wound!

BIXIO takes a cursory look, without getting up.

> BIXIO
>
> Scratch over the ribs... *(Calls to the SOLDIER)* Get some cobwebs for it! Poultice of cobwebs and dock leaves!

SOLDIER #2 staggers off uncertainly, dripping blood.

> CAMPION
>
> He seemed quite badly hurt.

> BIXIO
>
> Oh, he's only a Sicilian. Hullo...?

They both listen. CAMPION can hear nothing. He shakes his head.

> BIXIO
>
> Listen... *(They listen)*... There!...

> CAMPION
>
> *(Listens)*
>
> No... No, I can't. Wait a minute...

From a long way off, comes the sounds of shouting.

> BIXIO
>
> *(Laughs)*
>
> He's coming through the lines. Ha ha!
> Garibaldi! Garibaldi, si!

The cry gets louder. 'GARIBALDI, SI! is repeated, closer and closer.

Several SOLDIERS enter, their caps on their bayonets. They seem to be drunk and look villainous. SOLDIER #1 kicks CAMPION affectionately; SOLDIER #2 shoots wildly...causing CAMPION to hide under a log.

More SOLDIERS run on, shoving – dangerous in their vitality. SOLDIER #4 blows a cornet. There is firing, shouting and cheers.

ACT ONE

SOLDIERS

Garibaldi, si! Garibaldi, si! Garibaldi, si, si, si!

GARIBALDI enters. He wears a red shirt, a poncho, and carries a shotgun and a brace of pheasant. He throws it backwards over his shoulder. There's a rush for them. FRANCESCA gets the pheasants.

GARIBALDI

That's enough, boys, that's enough!

He whispers to SOLDIER #4, who nods and picks up a guitar.

To quieten the SOLDIERS, GARIBALDI sings a plaintive Italian folk song – 'Calabrisella mia.'

GARIBALDI

Nina ti vitti all'acqua chi lavavi ...
E lu me cori si jinchiu d'amuri.
Mentre li panni a la sipala 'ampravi
Io t'arrobbai lu megghiu muccaturi.
Calabrisella mia,
Calabrisella mia,
Calabrisella mia,
Facimmu amuri

BIXIO joins in.

Tirullalleru, lalleru lallà
'sta Calabrisella muriri mi fa!

SOLDIER #3 plays a concertina. GARIBALDI sings alone.

GARIBALDI

Mo chi di la città jeu su turnatu
Mi guardi e mi sorridi malandrina
Dassaria tuttu lu meu dutturato
Sulu p'aviri a tia sempri vicina.
Calabrisella mia,
Daria la me vita

> Calabrisella mia
> Sulu pe tia.

BIXIO joins in.

> Tirullalleru, lalleru lallà
> 'sta Calabrisella muriri mi fa!

GARIBALDI harmonizes on the last line.

> 'sta Calabrisella muriri mi fa!

Cheers. CAMPION applauds fervently. GARIBALDI sees him. SOLDIER #1 drags CAMPION forward.

SOLDIER #1
Hiding behind a tree, General.

GARIBALDI
Shoot him. No, don't waste a bullet! *(SOLDIER #1 takes out a fearsome knife)* Not here – we're going to eat! Do it over there. Damned rogue of an Austrian!

CAMPION
(As he is hauled away)
I'm not Austrian, General! I'm an Englishman. I'm here to interview you. I'm English!

GARIBALDI
English? English?! You're wearing a vile Austrian hat!

CAMPION
I'm sorry, I thought it suited me.

Laughter.

GARIBALDI
Oh, give him a bowl of soup.

FRANCESCA and the SEAMSTRESS bring the cauldron forward.

ACT ONE

GARIBALDI fills two bowls, gives them to the women, with a bow.

GARIBALDI

So, you're a journalist, Signor?

SOLDIER #2, breaks loaves of bread. A BOY SOLDIER serves soup to GARIBALDI and CAMPION, who sit down side by side.

CAMPION

I'm here from the London Times to interview you. General, may I cover your campaign? The world should know of the brave attempt of you and the gallant One Thousand to unite Italy.

GARIBALDI

Attempt? We shall!

The BOY SOLDIER serves the SOLDIERS, who are hungry and make a lot of noise eating.

GARIBALDI

So, you're a journalist, Signor?

GARIBALDI gestures to BIXIO, who throws CAMPION a hunk of bread. GARIBALDI waves for him to eat.

CAMPION

(Double-taking.)

Oh, yes.

GARIBALDI strikes a thoughtful pose.

GARIBALDI

Mine...has been a stormy life. Good and evil have been mixed, as I suppose they have in the lives of most men. Quiet – quiet!

He hits SOLDIER #2 over the head.

GARIBALDI
Do you wish to take notes?

CAMPION
Oh yes, General, thank you. Most obliged.

CAMPION takes up his book and pencil.

GARIBALDI
I can conscientiously say...that I have always sought...to act...rightly...both in fulfilling my duty...got that? And in seeking the good of others. I have always been the foe...no...correction...the Sworn foe... *(He glares ferociously at CAMPION)* of tyranny and falsehood, believing them...to be...the source of all human misery. New paragraph. I...am a Republican...such being the system for all sane men. However, I am not an intolerant man. If the English are content with the government of that good little woman, Victoria, then it goes to prove, that whatever they choose to call it... they have... a Republic.

CAMPION
I beg your pardon?

BIXIO
Don't interrupt the General.

CAMPION
I beg the General's pardon. No offence.

GARIBALDI
And none taken sir. None taken. *(He takes up his pose again.)* My life... has provided... and may continue to provide... material for history.

SOLDIERS
Hear, hear. Hear, hear!

ACT ONE

He notices CAMPION's camera equipment.

GARIBALDI

Is that your camera?

CAMPION

Yes, May I...?

GARIBALDI nods gracefully. CAMPION jumps up, and sets up his tripod. GARIBALDI stands, and takes up a pose, holding it as CAMPION messes about and, finally takes the picture. Cheers.

SOLDIERS

A song, General, a song!

GARIBALDI

What... a song?

He makes to take his singing stance but BIXIO gestures to CAMPION and he continues.

GARIBALDI

I have seen battles.

SOLDIERS

Hurray... hurray!

GARIBALDI

To those who have fallen, my loving respect. To the living – less so. But *(grinding his teeth)* I have always endeavoured to control righteous indignation.

He suddenly turns and smites the SOLDIER #5 behind him.

GARIBALDI

Dog!

SOLDIER #5 removes his hand from CAMPION's bag.

GARIBALDI

Where was I?

CAMPION

"... righteous indignation."

GARIBALDI

(Grinding his teeth again)

Ah! Yes!

CAMPION

Sir, my readers are eager to know why you and your followers wear red shirts.

GARIBALDI

Red shirts? We-ell...

SOLDIERS

For courage! Red for the fire of courage! The blood of the enemy! Garibaldi si – Garibaldi si! Garibaldi, si!

GARIBALDI smiles.

Blackout.

ACT ONE – SCENE FOUR

The island of Caprera. Day.

As the first scene. GARIBALDI and CAMPION. BIXIO has left

GARIBALDI

Pig's trotters.

CAMPION

I beg your pardon?

GARIBALDI

The shirts were left out of a consignment to Argentina. For the slaughterers to wear in the abattoirs.

ACT ONE

CAMPION pauses, pencil in hand.

> GARIBALDI
>
> No need to write that down.

FRANCESCA enters, a live chicken under each arm. She stands before them, her face fearsome.

> GARIBALDI
>
> *(Nudges CAMPION)*
>
> Well? You're the guest!

> CAMPION
>
> I'm sorry?

> GARIBALDI
>
> Choose, man. A chicken in your honour. Which one?

CAMPION tries, but shakes his head.

> CAMPION
>
> Tell the Signora I leave it in her capable hands.

FRANCESCA looks to GARIBALDI in enquiry.

> GARIBALDI
>
> He honours you with the choice, heart of my life. For your wisdom and beauty.

FRANCESCA stamps off. There is a terrible squawk as a hen is killed.

> CAMPION
>
> May we continue? If I could prompt your memory, beloved General. The world must have a record of the bravest man I have ever known.

> GARIBALDI
>
> That's true. I've never met a man braver than the man who sits here before you.

CAMPION

People need to know, General. So they may have an example of a great military hero upon which to model themselves.

GARIBALDI

Really? *(He leans forward, and looks at CAMPION keenly.)* Tell me something, Campion. Have you a son?

CAMPION shakes his head.

GARIBALDI

If you had a son – would you send him for a soldier?

CAMPION gazes at him, and shudders.

GARIBALDI

No.

CAMPION

I'm sorry.

GARIBALDI

Why? Natural feelings? Never easy, recruitment.

CAMPION

I remember.

Light change.

ACT ONE – SCENE FIVE

The encampment. We are back on the campaign.

An ARTIST is drawing GARIBALDI. GARIBALDI sits at a table, with GENERAL FRANCESCO CRISPI beside him.

CAMPION sits apart, to observe.

ACT ONE

CRISPI

Next!

A YOUNG BOY enters, clutching his hat.

CRISPI

Name?

BOY

Andreotti.

CRISPI

Sign here. *(The BOY bends, signs.)* Date of birth?

BOY

1845. I am twenty years old, General Crispi.

CRISPI

And you were born fifteen years ago.

BOY

I have learned to write, Signor, but not arithmetic.

GARIBALDI

(Growls)

Send him home to his mother.

CRISPI jerks his head. The YOUNG BOY goes. CRISPI beckons. A YOUNG MAN (VALERI) enters, tall, handsome, well-dressed. Bows twice with a flourish, turns to bow to CAMPION but SOLDIER #1 pushes him back towards the table.

VALERI

Giovanni Valeri, at your service, General Crispi.

CRISPI

Age?

VALERI

Twenty.

GARIBALDI
Put his name down.

CRISPI
Report to the sergeant.

VALERI
Bravo!

He throws his hat in the air, dances off in excitement. GARIBALDI looks after him, disenchanted.

CAMPION
A fine man, General.

GARIBALDI
A dead man, eh? *(To CRISPI, who nods.)*

CAMPION
I'm sorry?

GARIBALDI
By good fortune he doesn't know it.

CRISPI
Bad for morale when they do.

CAMPION
It doesn't worry you – that a young man may lose his life?

GARIBALDI
(Thinks, shrugs)
I'm sorry for his mother. As for dying ...

CRISPI
Same for us all.

ACT ONE

GARIBALDI

...anyway, who believes the shell fragment's for his liver at twenty?

CAMPION

But you are not twenty, gentlemen. Does not the thought of death – your own deaths...?

GARIBALDI

(Jumps up, eyes blazing)

What matters, Englishman, is what you're prepared to die for! I – Giuseppe Garibaldi – believe in Freedom! In a united, independent Italy!

CRISPI

To have a cause more important than your own life.

GARIBALDI

We die! Every man, every woman on God's earth. So, do we creep around like lice? This glorious world – for a short time – ours! And then – phtt! – no trace. Who, soon enough, is left to remember our name?

CAMPION

Tout lasse – tout passe, as the French say.

GARIBALDI

So, why love your children, desire your wife? Why feel anything? I feel, Englishman. Here! A burning desire.

CRISPI

For Freedom!

He looks over the ARTIST's shoulder.

GARIBALDI

Make me handsomer.

CAMPION

I agree. But perhaps – for most of us – freedom is to be pursued in the personal. In the achievement of decency in private life.

GARIBALDI

A private life is a luxury – to be won – if necessary, with blood.

BIXIO enters.

BIXIO

We're ready to move off.

The GARIBALDINI (SOLDIERS) cross the stage with their gear.

GARIBALDI and CRISPI begin a deep in discussion and exit. CAMPION is left alone, bewildered at the swift decampment. Their voices die away.

Fade to black.

ACT ONE – SCENE SIX

The court of King Victor Emmanuel.

The elegant sound of salon music. A dance is in progress offstage, watched by VICTOR EMMANUEL, King of Piedmont, and PRINCE METTERNICH, the Austrian Chancellor. CAVOUR, the King's Minister, stands discreetly nearby. The dance ends to polite applause.

METTERNICH, irritated by the music, shows satisfaction as it stops. He turns to the KING.

ACT ONE

METTERNICH

As I was attempting to say, Majesty – to pound ten kingdoms into one Italy is, in the opinion of the Austrian Empire, impossible. There is no such realm – no such place – no such country on the map. What we have are a collection of small states – to be handled, administered, and dealt with separately.

KING

We lack your Austrian discipline, Chancellor.

CAVOUR

(Aside) Bollocks. *(Aloud)* Absolutely. Keep the states weak and separated. Anyway, south of Rome – dry rock. As for Sicily, that turd on the end of the boot . . . *(He shrugs eloquently.)*

METTERNICH

Precisely. The French . . .

CAVOUR

(Quick)

Oh, nothing going on there.

KING

Where we are concerned, the status quo is, ah . . .

CAVOUR

Nothing going on with the French – nothing at all.

METTERNICH rises. He looks dangerous.

METTERNICH

I acknowlodge your reassurances. Any alteration to international stability we would take very seriously.

He bows – steps back – bows again and goes.

CAVOUR

Doesn't Metternich know?

KING

That the one clear chance of a united Italy lies in hatred of Austria? It seems not. But he's right. We're no threat.

CAVOUR

(Smiles)

It doesn't do to forget that a mosquito can kill a man, Sire.

KING

Well said.

CAVOUR

On the subject of which, there's that tiresome rabble-rouser. Do we wish to see him? *(Hands a paper to the KING.)*

KING

(Reads)

Garibaldi ... What does he want?

CAVOUR

Muskets. Carbines. Cannon. With which to topple you.

KING

Send him away.

CAVOUR

(Brightening)

To be disposed of?

KING

That's your affair.

Cheering, off.

ACT ONE

CAVOUR

They've been there for three days.

KING

In the red shirts? *(CAVOUR nods.)* Braising pigeons?

CAVOUR

I'll order their removal. At once.

KING

No. Have them in.

CAVOUR

Here? Now?

KING

Why not?

CAVOUR, scowling, whispers to his aide, CAPTAIN ETTORE ASTI, who goes out. Sounds of Court Music offstage. Cheering, off.

GARIBALDI enters, followed by SIX GARIBALDIANS. Consternation from the COURT. One LADY screams. A flame-haired MARQUESA drops her fan. She backs away as GARIBALDI advances on her. He picks up her fan, presents it to her with a bow, and escorts her to a seat, pulling it out for her. He bows again, kisses her hand.

Whispering and a little applause. GARIBALDI approaches the KING who rises and descends to meet him. He embraces him.

KING

You know Cavour, of course.

GARIBALDI

I do.

CAVOUR comes forward, claps GARIBALDI on the shoulder.

CAVOUR

The General knows I am his greatest admirer.

GARIBALDI is flattered.

KING

You've got some good dinner roasting outside, General.

GARIBALDI

Come and join us.

KING

I will.

ASTI whispers in CAVOUR's ear. CAVOUR whispers in the KING's ear.

KING

He says it's raining. Send out some platters. We'll eat under cover, eh?

CAVOUR nods to ASTI, who goes. Some cheering off.

KING

Now General ...

GARIBALDI makes to unroll a map, looks round for space, clears a table of ornaments and flowers at a swoop – to screeches from the LADIES – and unrolls his map.

GARIBALDI

As I see it ...

CAVOUR

As we see it, the Kingdom of Piedmont, which is our responsibility.

GARIBALDI

Piedmont? That's only the top of Italy.

ACT ONE

CAVOUR

Italy? What is Italy?

Noise as the platters of food are brought in and handed round. The KING eats with his fingers, so members of the COURT do the same. GARIBALDI serves the LADIES.

CAVOUR

(To the KING)

Sire – don't mention that Savoy and Nice are to be ceded to France. *(Nods at GARIBALDI.)* Nice is his home.

KING

But if we need popular support, and he's the man to get it, hang on to Nice for him.

CAVOUR

The French won't have it, and we need their support against Austria.

GARIBALDI returns, offers food to CAVOUR who eats a chicken leg held in a white napkin – with ASTI to hand with a finger bowl. The LADIES are charmed by the YOUNG GARIBALDIANS.

KING

(To GARIBALDI)

You know what the Austrians call you, General? Rosheufel. Red Devil.

This is whispered around the COURT – "The Red Devil." The KING claps. More clapping. MUSIC. The GARIBALDIANS dance a Soldiers Dance over their swords then dance with the LADIES to the waltz.

SIGNOR B comes up behind METTERNICH.

SIGNOR B

Huzza!

METTERNICH

Are you addressing me?

SIGNOR B

The waltz – the waltz eh? Strong stuff – ha ha, you Austrians! *(He mimes dancing with his arms around a partner.)* Strong stuff!

METTERNICH

Who is this man?

BIXIO

(Calls to GARIBALDI)

Your father's annoying the Prince.

GARIBALDI

(Calls)

He's not my father. I thought he was yours!

SIGNOR B

(In METTERNICH'S ear)

That Prince Metternich – is it true that he worships the ground under his own feet?

BIXIO drags SIGNOR B away as METTERNICH, furious, goes.

CAVOUR

Damn!

He hurries after METTERNICH.

Blackout.

ACT ONE

ACT ONE – SCENE SEVEN

An ante room in the King's palace. Night.

MUSIC, offstage. GARIBALDI and the KING, with CAVOUR in the background, watching them.

> GARIBALDI
>
> What we need, King, is guns. For myself I prefer the bayonet, but the youngsters like to make a noise.

> KING
>
> We'll see what we can do.

> GARIBALDI
>
> I promise them weariness, hardship and battle. And I keep my promises. Do you keep yours?

> KING
>
> I've said so. You'll have your weapons.

CAVOUR, in the background, glares, and walks away.

> KING
>
> Very able man, Cavour.

> GARIBALDI
>
> The wingless swan.

> KING
>
> *(Laughs)*
>
> I'm not absolutely sure to what extent I value his opinions. Still – an intelligent and resourceful man. A prick of course.

> GARIBALDI
>
> And not in favour of a United Italy.

KING

He thinks it impractical. From the political point of view.

GARIBALDI

So, no go?

KING

I didn't say that. I – Victor Emmanuel – share your aims. We think alike. One Italy! On a par with France and Spain. Nation countries with natural boundaries. To hell with oppressive empires, eh?

GARIBALDI
(Charmed)

You are right!

KING

Every man a citizen of his own land. "I am an Italian."

GARIBALDI

Bravo! Bravo!

KING

Here's what we'll do. They won't give you the army, they don't trust you. But you can raise volunteers.

GARIBALDI

Volunteers? The best! There's no discipline like conviction! What about arms, victuals?

KING

Leave it to me. *(He shakes GARIBALDI's hand.)*

GARIBALDI goes. CAVOUR enters.

KING

Ah, Cavour. I had to offer him something.

ACT ONE

CAVOUR

Of course, Sire. Volunteers. That should keep him busy.

KING

He's good with men.

CAVOUR

Perhaps out of the main arena? For safety's sake?

KING

Mmm.

CAVOUR

The protection of Your Majesty's Kingdom of Northern Italy is my sole concern.

KING

Which you perform admirably. None better.

CAVOUR

Even pricks have their uses.

KING

Pardon – I should have lowered our voice. Just leading him on to get his drift.

CAVOUR

What did he mean – wingless swan?

KING

No idea.

CAVOUR

He'll need to be watched.

KING

See to it. *(Goes)*

CAVOUR beckons CAPTAIN ASTI.

CAVOUR

Take this down. We commit to the employment of Garibaldi in the raising of volunteer troops against Austria. But there is to be no money – no food – no uniforms – above all, no arms.

They start to leave.

CAVOUR

Don't allow him to operate anywhere near military objectives and keep his name out of the papers. With a bit of luck, he'll fall off his horse, eh?

They go. The KING enters, followed by CAPTAIN ASTI.

KING

Take this down. General Garibaldi to be furnished with three ships – to be sent to Sicily. The ships to carry ordnance – guns, carbines, muskets, ammunition, and swords – uniforms, dry foods and boots. See to it.

ASTI

Very good, sir.

The KING goes. CAVOUR enters.

ASTI

What am I to do?

CAVOUR

Nothing.

ASTI

I can't do nothing!

CAVOUR
(Irritable)

All right. Find a couple of ships. Preferably suicidal tubs held together by the sea they float on.

ACT ONE

ASTI

Sorry?

CAVOUR

I want ships that are leaky – wobbly – whatever ships do when they're not ... *(looks for word)*

ASTI

Seaworthy? What do you want done with them?

CAVOUR

Mend them!

ASTI

You mean, put them in for refit?

CAVOUR

Refit, poor fit, epileptic fit, whatever takes the longest!

ASTI

His Majesty's not a fool. He'll be after me.

CAVOUR

So, do the repairs!

ASTI

And the cargo?

CAVOUR

Don't tell me you can't lay your hands on some obsolete weapons.

ASTI

You want rubbish? *(CAVOUR nods)* Just so I have it clear. We are not looking at Garibaldi, despite all this public support, as an ally?

CAVOUR

(*Indignant*)

The man's a Republican!

ASTI

And the King?

CAVOUR

The King finds Garibaldi charming. Since he himself, like most monarchs, survives on charm, he esteems it in others.

ASTI

Two of a kind, you're saying?

CAVOUR

Blood brothers, Captain. (*As they go*) I've nothing against Garibaldi personally. A simple soul.

ASTI

The women like him.

They go.

Light change.

ACT ONE – SCENE EIGHT

In the Field.

Noise. Shouts, yells, screams – men running – fighting hand to hand – the neighing of horses – groans – the sound of cannon and carbines. Smoke everywhere obscures the action.

ACT ONE

GARIBALDI

(Offstage)

Forward! Forward! Don't let them catch you flat-a-back!

As the smoke clears, the sounds die away. SOLDIER #1 – wounded – limps across the stage. SOLDIER #2 helps on wounded SOLDIER #3. SOLDIERS #4 and #5 pull on a painted Sicilian cart with the BOY SOLDIER lying in the back, his face deathly pale. GENERAL FRANCESCO CRISPI enters with CAPTAIN SILVIO BARBONE. They consult a list.

CRISPI

Altieri?

BARBONE

Dead.

CRISPI

Rossato?

BARBONE

Wounded.

CRISPI

Villanova?

The CAPTAIN shrugs. He doesn't know. GARIBALDI enters. He looks round, throws his haversack to a group of SOLDIERS. They wave thanks, take out the bread, and eat.

GARIBALDI

I need a man on the right flank.

CRISPI

Yes. *(Indicates the list. GARIBALDI takes it and reads.)* Gordiano?

217

GARIBALDI
Too slow.

CRISPI
Young Marchetti?

GARIBALDI
Sixteen?

BARBONE
(Stabs at the list))
Strozzi!

CRISPI
(Agreeing)
Ah!

GARIBALDI
(Shakes his head)
No, no.

CRISPI
Why not? He's alive.

BARBONE
Unwounded.

CRISPI
You can't find fault with his ardour for the fight.

GARIBALDI
No.

CRISPI
Why?

They look at him.

GARIBALDI
He likes killing.

ACT ONE

> BARBONE
>
> General – I don't mean to contradict, or say what you've just said is – is – *(GARIBALDI glares at him)* It doesn't make no sense!
>
> GARIBALDI
>
> No sense? No sense? What do you think you are? What are you?
>
> BARBONE
>
> A soldier!
>
> GARIBALDI
> *(To everyone)*
>
> And what are soldiers?
>
> SOLDIERS
>
> Fighters! We're here to fight the enemy, General! We're here to win – fight. Fighting! Garibaldi, si!

GARIBALDI shakes his head, puts up his hand for silence.

> CRISPI
>
> No?
>
> GARIBALDI
>
> No.
>
> CRISPI
>
> A soldier is not for fighting?
>
> GARIBALDI
>
> I didn't say that.

He sits, then gets up and walks about.

> GARIBALDI
>
> What is a man?

SOLDIER #2

Me, sir.

GARIBALDI

What is his purpose?

SOLDIER #2

Fighting?

GARIBALDI

I'll tell you what his purpose is.

SOLDIER #4

I wish you would.

GARIBALDI

(*Flooring him with an upper cut*)

I will – I will. The purpose of a man ... The purpose of a man is fornication.

Laughter and cheering.

GARIBALDI

You think I'm joking? You think that I – Giuseppe Garibaldi – your leader, the leader of the gallant One Thousand – who will take Naples, take Rome – you think I make jokes about the rights and purpose of man? I am not a joker. I am a serious man.

Murmurs of agreement.

GARIBALDI

Why do I say that a man is made to fornicate? Think! Consider! To fornicate is to be a man.

SOLDIER #2

Prove your manhood!

SOLDIER #5

Show your mettle!

ACT ONE

SOLDIER #4 crows like a cock.

GARIBALDI

Yes – get the paddle out – in and out – up the spout and into the oven. The purpose of a man is to fill a woman. *(Murmurs of agreement.)* Life. His only function. Life. To create – and to protect – life. Think of it my friends. There she stands, the woman – lovely, shining – in all her glory ... And to what does that Venus – that Aphrodite – submit? Why, to the invasion of her very self – from without by a man – from within by the child of her womb.

SOLDIERS

True – true – that's so!

CRISPI

Well said.

GARIBALDI

You talk of courage – the sapper in the tunnel – the charge at the enemy. Ever seen a woman in labour, son?

SOLDIER #2 shakes his head.

GARIBALDI

A soldier exists to honour life. He is for the protection of his wife – his children – his neighbour's children – thereby his country – and therefore – not one life to be wasted! We are fighters – not killers. Persuade when possible, evade where able, bypass, circumvent, advance nonetheless – kill only in defence of the life of your friend – and to save your own skin. I speak seriously. From the heart. In this campaign, never forget. When you kill an Italian, you kill your brother.

SOLDIER #1

(Pause)

What about foreigners?

GARIBALDI

Foreigners? Foreigners? Tell them to clear off, or you'll blow their brains out!

Laughter. FRANCESCA and the SEAMSTRESS carry a cauldron across the stage. The SOLDIERS follow them off eagerly. Only GARIBALDI and CRISPI are left. They smoke their pipes.

CRISPI

Ah – women! Women. Ahhh! Can't do without 'em, eh?

GARIBALDI nods, puffs at his pipe.

CRISPI

For me it's the arse.

They smoke in silence.

CRISPI

Not that there's anything like a good bosom. A good bosom, spilling out of a dress. *(Pause)* Mind you, nothing wrong with a good tush. Good tush on a woman and you're away. There are those who wouldn't give you two lire one way or the other so long as it's there. Not me. For me – a good arse. I've never met a mean woman with a good bum. If you want a good woman, I say take look at her bum. The bum first and foremost.

GARIBALDI

What about the face?

CRISPI

Oh, I never look at that.

ACT ONE

Offstage the SOLDIERS singing "Addio, mia Bella, Addio."

GARIBALDI picks up the tune, sings the verses. The SOLDIERS drift on, singing the choruses.

                GARIBALDI + SOLDIERS

Addio, mia bella, addio
l'armata se ne va
se non partissi anch'io
sarebbe una viltà.

Non pianger, mio tesoro,
forse ritornerò;
ma se in battaglia io moro
in ciel ti rivedrò.

La spada, le pistole,
lo schioppo li ho con me:
all'apparir del sole
mi partirò da te!

Il sacco preparato
sull'òmero mi sta;
son uomo e son soldato:
viva la libertà!

son uomo e son soldato:
viva la libertà!

Lights slow fade to black.

ACT ONE – SCENE 9

Naples. Loud cheering.

In the background, TWO SAILORS wave from the rigging.

GARIBALDI, SI!

THREE MEN, THREE WOMEN, and a BOY crane to see GARIBALDI.

A MAN reels, and falls to the ground.

> ENGLISH PROFESSOR
> *(To a WOMAN)*
> What is it? Has he had a turn?

> WOMAN
> No, Englishman! He feels Joy. Joy – to be free! You are
> English, how can you understand? *(Shouts)* Garibaldi
> si! Garibaldi si!

The cry is taken up. 'Garibaldi, si!' Garibaldi, si!' The SAILORS and PEOPLE wave. The BOY jumps up and down.

Deafening cheers as GARIBALDI arrives, standing in an open carriage drawn by excited CIVILIANS. BIXIO, his aide, is at his side.

> BIXIO
> Sit down, there are still Bourbon troops up there!

> GARIBALDI
> You think they will shoot? With this going on?

He acknowledges the crowds without flamboyance, then waves his hands for silence.

> GARIBALDI
> Dear friends. This is the day on which a new history
> begins for Italy – and for its finest town – Naples!

Cheers, flags wave, a few carbines let off into the air.

> GARIBALDI
> I thank you for your welcome, on behalf of Italy, which,
> with your help, will be a free and united country!

Cheers.

Blackout.

ACT ONE – SCENE TEN

The Island of Caprera.

After dinner. FRANCESCA, scowling, enters with a flagon of wine and a tray, and takes away the remains of dinner. GARIBALDI pours wine for himself and CAMPION. The SPY sneaks out, proffering his empty wineglass. CAMPION indicates: shall he refill the spy's glass?

> GARIBALDI
> No, no, no – he won't find his way home.
>
> CAMPION
> Naples! It must have been amazing. An extraordinary experience.
>
> GARIBALDI
> It was. *(He lights his pipe.)*
>
> CAMPION
> What, may I ask, is your clearest memory?
>
> GARIBALDI
> The women.
>
> CAMPION
> The women?
>
> GARIBALDI
> Not a woman in Naples – young, old – who didn't offer herself.
>
> CAMPION
> And did you …?

GARIBALDI shakes his head.

GARIBALDI

Too busy. Anyway, we needed cooks and nurses – not lovers.

GARIBALDI takes a drink. A pause. He puffs his pipe.

CAMPION

General – *(clears his throat.)* May I ask you a question?

GARIBALDI turns, and looks at him.

CAMPION

Do you like fighting?

GARIBALDI

(After a pause)

No sir. The cost is always too great. For a man in my position – no battle is ever won. At best, it is not lost.

CAMPION

As in Naples?

GARIBALDI

You saw us there! *(Laughs.)*

CAMPION

No sir – it was in Rome that we met again.

GARIBALDI

Ah Rome! Rome!

Light change.

ACT ONE – SCENE ELEVEN

Rome.

ACT ONE

MAZZINI and the MAYOR on the platform. The MAYOR takes a formal stance, head erect, one foot forward.

> **MAYOR**
> Signor Mazzini! *(A lone cheer.)* With open and brimming hearts – we welcome you to Rome. To Rome – the Eternal City!

Some applause.

> **MAYOR**
> Rome – the centre of civilisation – of the world – is enriched by your respected, your beloved – may I say – holy presence.

MAZZINI, seated at his side, shakes his head modestly.

> **MAYOR**
> On this auspicious day, at this glorious moment, with one great deliverer on the ramparts already – his troops approaching – I speak of none other than General Giuseppe Garibaldi *(wild cheers)* we are doubly honoured – our humility and gratitude know no bounds.

Cheers throughout.

> **MAYOR**
> We give thanks to the Almighty for the courage of the General and his gallant One Thousand men who have liberated Sicily – and Naples – and now Rome. And made it possible for us to welcome here, in our midst – the core, the heart of the movement for the unification of our beloved country. Ladies and gentlemen, I give you – the heart and soul of Italy – its champion – Signor Giuseppe Mazzini!

Applause. MAZZINI rises, and waits for silence.

MAZZINI
This is a momentous day. Particularly for those of us who have worked for the uniting of Italy for thirty years. To be regarded for thirty years as an insane agitator can be tiring to the spirit. Not to mention being that devil with horns – a Republican. I am not – despite rumour – a communist. To replace an ancien regime, an emperor, with another dictatorship – a new enslavement – can that be human progress? Decency in human affairs can only – in my opinion – be secured by two elemental ideas. First, by nationalism. What is a nation? A nation is a grouping of people defined by natural boundaries – the sea, rivers, mountains, and by language. By customs. By traditions long evolved. What is the alternative? Foreign domination? Aggressive tribalism? Or – instead – a mindless, shapeless spread of people, encouraged by the new ease of travel, to abandon their countries – where they are needed – to seek fresh territory. A dissemination dominated by the predatory aspects of trade, and exploitation by the new commercial colonialism. A nation provides stability, protection, opportunity. *(Applause.)* Most men want no more than a fair share, and the respect of their peers. Man has survived by a sense of fairness. And how is that survival best protected? By the second elemental idea after nationalism. The principle of Democracy. One man! One vote!

Loud applause. The MAYOR and MAZZINI go. CAVOUR enters, followed by ASTI.

CAVOUR
Has he finished?

ACT ONE

                    ASTI

Mazzini? Yes.

                    CAVOUR

We were assured he was still abroad. Has the King
arrived?

                    ASTI

I'll find out.

He goes quickly. CAVOUR strides up and down.

The KING enters, followed by ASTI.

                    KING

Cavour?

CAVOUR, startled, jumps – then bends the knee.

                    CAVOUR

Thank you for coming so promptly, Sire.

                    KING

Your messages conveyed unusual urgency.

CAVOUR nods to ASTI, who lets down the large map of Italy.

                    CAVOUR
                (Takes pointer from ASTI)
Our Kingdom – your Kingdom, Sire. Sardinia,
Piedmont. As you know, there has never been
objection to the annexation of Lombardy – even –
notwithstanding the Austrians – Tuscany and
Venetia – fertile, profitable, containable and
manageable adjuncts to your Majesty's realm.

                    KING

What about France?

KING

Anything to spite Austria.

KING

What is your point?

CAVOUR

My point is – the Papal States, the kingdom of Naples – Apulia – Calabria – and Sicily.

KING

As you so often say, fit only for goats since we cut down all the trees to build railways.

CAVOUR

I've been giving the matter some thought. As is my responsibility as your chancellor. If Rome is taken – remains taken – the Pope has already left the city – then the Papal States – here – and here – go begging.

KING

And who is most likely to –?

CAVOUR

The French. Their troops are installed here. As for the rest, I begin to see advantage in Garibaldi.

KING

Garibaldi? The romantic?

CAVOUR

No. Mazzini is the romantic. Believes in human virtue. Garibaldi's more of a realist. I've been corresponding with him.

KING

Have you?

ACT ONE

CAVOUR

As you have, Sire.

CAVOUR nods to ASTI, who rolls up the map.

CAVOUR

One map, one country. One language – no more impenetrable dialects. One currency – no more borders, and customs officers with open palms. One monetary, economic, political...

KING

And cultural...

CAVOUR

Unit. Precisely. *(Silence.)* King of Italy. On a par with France – England and her navy.

KING

You said the South would eat money.

CAVOUR

It's survived so far. Let it take care of itself, as before. As a barrier against invasion.

KING

Italy but not Italy?

CAVOUR

Oh Italy, beyond a doubt. Italian language – Italian law...

The whine of a bullet. They duck.

KING

Rome – it appears – is still not taken. Where's Garibaldi?

CAVOUR

We were assured he was on the ramparts.

Sounds of battle. GARIBALDI, wounded, is brought in hurriedly on a litter by SOLDIERS #1 and #2, followed by CRISPI.

GARIBALDI

No – no – no!

CRISPI

Don't be a fool, Giuseppe! Give the order to withdraw!

GARIBALDI

No!

MAZZINI enters.

MAZZINI

We must vacate the premises. *(Shots – they duck.)*
Please – Sir, come away – at least to the cellars.

CAVOUR

Yes, yes, yes. Come –

KING

What about the General?

CRISPI

We'll get you down the stairs.

GARIBALDI hits out at him.

GARIBALDI

Get off, Crispi! What's the matter with you?

CAVOUR and MAZZINI duck at a rattling sound.

CRISPI

Come on!

ACT ONE

CAVOUR
That was close.

MAZZINI
Are they snipers?

GARIBALDI
Snipers? Snipers? I'll tell you what they are? Men with sling shots!

CRISPI
You mean ...

GARIBALDI
I mean they've run out of ammunition! They're throwing stones!

GARIBALDINI erupt into the room, victorious.

Fade to black.

ACT ONE – SCENE 12

Rome

MUSIC. The celebration of the conquest of Rome. A CARDINAL gives a religious blessing in Latin.

CARDINAL
(Makes the sign of the cross)
Salve Regina, Mater misericordiae. Vita, dulcedo, et spes nostra, salve. Ad te clamamus exsules filii Hevae. Ad te Suspiramus, gementes et flentes in hac lacrimarum valle. Eia ergo, Advocata nostra, illos tuos misericordes oculos as nos converte. Et Iesum, benedictum fructum ventris tui, nobis post

hoc exsilium ostende. O Clemens, o pia, o dulcis Virgo
Maria. Amen

Present are MAZZINI, CAVOUR, and the KING. GARIBALDI, on a litter, is flanked by the MARQUESA and JESSIE, in a nurse's uniform.

Some jealousy between the women. Cheers, flags and singing. BIXIO enters with a long piece of paper. GARIBALDI looks up at him. He bends down. GARIBALDI whispers in his ear. BIXIO steps forward, and begins to read the list.

BIXIO

Mario Acerbori

Pietro Adarno

Luciano Addario

Maurizio Addoloni

Michele Adorni

Marcello Agazia

Michele Agiolli

Bruno Alagna

Antonio Albanese

Sandro Alberi

Daniele Albertani

Slowly the cheering and shouting die away.

CARBONE steps forward with another long list.

CARBONE

Pietro Albrizzi

Giorgio Aldegani

Antonio Alesini

Oliviero Alesini

Giulio Alesini

Now there is silence.

ACT ONE

CARBONE

Giuseppe Alfare

Marco Allafini

Angelo Altieri

Benito Alvini

The light begins to go until only their voices are heard.

BIXIO

Michelangelo Amadi

Luigi Amianti

Bruno Andreani

Beppo Andreani

Daniele Arcangeli

Ernesto Armano

Paolo Astori

Emiliano Baggi

Lights to black.

END OF ACT ONE

ACT TWO

ACT TWO – SCENE ONE

A simple room. Day.

GARIBALDI, convalescent, in a narrow cot. BIXIO, by his bed, reads from his list.

>> BIXIO
> Enrico Pavanelli
> Vincenzo Pedrali
> Pietro Rizzi
> Leandro Poleti
> Enrico Puglia
> Mario Rafaele
> Cristiano Ranzato
> Emilio Salmasi
> Claudio Salvadori
> Bruno Salviati
> Ettore Salviati
> Paolo Salviati

>> GARIBALDI

Same family?

>> BIXIO
> Yes, General.

JESSIE, a Scottish nurse, enters with tray

>> JESSIE
> What are you doing here? No visitors allowed.

ACT TWO

> BIXIO
> *(Bows)*
> General Bixio, Signorina. Here on the General's orders.

> JESSIE
> Out, man. I give the orders here.

BIXIO is so surprised that he goes.

> GARIBALDI
> I see you have a way with generals!

> JESSIE
> *(Sadistically)*
> Let's take a look at that foot.

She treats his foot. GARIBALDI winces.

> JESSIE
> What was yon man reading to you? You're supposed to be resting.

> GARIBALDI
> The list of our casualties.

> JESSIE
> Well he can stop that.

> GARIBALDI
> I am responsible for their lives.

> JESSIE
> Not any more you're not. They're God's concern now.

> GARIBALDI
> Ow!

JESSIE

Don't be such a baby. *(She bends to smell his wound.)*
That smells better. It looks as though the maggots
have done their work.

GARIBALDI turns his head away, as JESSIE picks out the maggots.

JESSIE

On the other hand, if you're so concerned, you can
sign this.

She takes a paper from her pocket.

GARIBALDI

What is it?

JESSIE

A requisition order for the Palace over yonder. I need
it for the wounded.

He holds up his hand for the paper. She gives him pen and ink.
He signs. She puts the paper in her pocket, and then dabs his
wound from a large bottle of purple liquid. He hollers. She bandages
him swiftly, gives him water, straightens his pillows, refills his
glass, and puts it by his bed.

JESSIE

You'll do. Tomorrow, on your feet.

She takes her tray and goes. BIXIO enters

GARIBALDI

Is there anything like a nurse? Prim as a snowdrop,
knows every bone of a man's body. I'll have her if it
costs me Sardinia.

He jumps as MAZZINI, behind BIXIO, coughs discreetly in the
doorway. He is holding a carbine. GARIBALDI gestures wildly to

ACT TWO

BIXIO, but he shrugs and goes. MAZZINI approaches and parks his carbine.

GARIBALDI

Mazzini – my friend! What's this? Come to do me an injury?

MAZZINI

In case we are attacked.

GARIBALDI

(As the gun clatters to the ground)

Other way up.

MAZZINI places the gun carefully. Then gives GARIBALDI a bunch of drooping flowers.

MAZZINI

No scent, I'm afraid.

GARIBALDI

Very nice.

GARIBALDI struggles to sit up. MAZZINI tries ineffectively to help him. GARIBALDI brushes him away, and shoves the flowers into a water glass.

GARIBALDI

What's happening?

MAZZINI

The general consensus of opinion is that one of us – you or I – must take over the running of Rome – as senator, mayor, leader.

GARIBALDI

Fancy the job?

MAZZINI

They'd prefer you.

GARIBALDI

Not my berth.

MAZZINI

If I could depend on your support ...

GARIBALDI

Of course!

MAZZINI

Thank you. And I'd value your advice on some practical matters. *(He leans forward, knocking into GARIBALDI's bad leg. GARIBALDI winces.)* I need your assistance, to begin with, on thirty-six points of information ...

MAZZINI forages among his bundle of papers. BIXIO looks in.

GARIBALDI gestures at him urgently.

GARIBALDI

(Hisses)

Get him out!

BIXIO

Apologies Signor Mazzini. The doctor is here, General, to remove your stitches.

He looms over MAZZINI menacingly. MAZZINI rises, scrapes back his chair.

MAZZINI

So sorry, do forgive me. Stitches?

ACT TWO

BIXIO

(Nods)

A bayonet wound.

MAZZINI

Oh – where?

BIXIO whispers in his ear. MAZZINI blenches.

MAZZINI

General, forgive me. Is it – are you –?

BIXIO

We're hoping for the best.

GARIBALDI

(Puts out his hand)

Another time, my friend.

MAZZINI bows and goes.

GARIBALDI

What did you tell him! *(They laugh.)*

BIXIO

Fellow's a fool.

GARIBALDI

Nonetheless, the most virtuous man in Italy.

BIXIO

(Wheeling GARIBALDI offstage)

What good's virtue in the pages of a book?

GARIBALDI

More than one sort of courage, Nino.

Blackout.

ACT TWO – SCENE TWO

The Island of Caprera.

GARIBALDI moves to ease his rheumatism.

>GARIBALDI
>And he left his gun behind.

CAMPION smiles.

>CAMPION
>But you respect Mazzini...

>GARIBALDI
>The father of us all! It was because of Mazzini...

He reaches for his cup, drops it. CAMPION retrieves it.

>CAMPION
>*(Shocked)*
>The marks – on your wrists?!

>GARIBALDI
>From the Rio Grande. Vile despots! Hung us up for hours! Hands the size of a bull's arse for months.

>CAMPION
>This was when you were exiled as a Republican?

>GARIBALDI
>Had to take the first ship I could find out of Nice to avoid arrest.

>CAMPION
>Where was it bound?

>GARIBALDI
>Russia. Very cold. After that – everywhere. Best men in the world, the mercantiles. In the end, I fetched up

ACT TWO

in South America, fitted out a small craft called 'The
Mazzini' – and fought for the Rio Grande Republicans.
You know what wins battles, Campion?

CAMPION shakes his head.

GARIBALDI

Chance. Chance and endurance. Never give up.

He goes silent. CAMPION makes rapid notes.

FRANCESCA emerges from the house with a tray with wine, two wine glasses and a pitcher of milk. She refills GARIBALDI's cup with milk, and fills a glass with wine, then crosses with it towards the flat rock by the thicket. She peers, looking for the SPY.

GARIBALDI

(To FRANCESCA)

It's Thursday. He's gone home to see his wife.

She returns and gives the glass of wine to CAMPION, with a bow.

CAMPION

Grazie.

She goes. CAMPION, at a cordial gesture from GARIBALDI to drink, lifts the glass of wine as a toast.

CAMPION

To General Garibaldi – a unique human being.

GARIBALDI

No, sir! I am an ordinary man. Of the common herd.

CAMPION

From whence sprang Columbus – Galileo – Titian,
Michelangelo – da Vinci!

GARIBALDI

And regiments of rogues. Ever seen men sack a town, Campion?

CAMPION

Never, thank God.

GARIBALDI

Beasts. Wild beasts. I had to put my own men to the sabre once. My own comrades. Men with families. *(Silence.)* That was in Uruguay. They wanted me to be Dictator.

CAMPION

You could still be King of Italy.

GARIBALDI shakes his head.

GARIBALDI

No, Campione.

He rises, going.

GARIBALDI

Never. I told them in Rome.

Blackout.

ACT TWO – SCENE THREE

The Streets of Rome and Palace balcony.

The night is lit by many candles. TOWNSFOLK and PEASANTS are waiting. A CHILD is on his FATHER's shoulders. The GARIBALDINI and FRENCH SOLDIERS are not friendly to one another. The SOUND OF A BAND playing a march approaches.

ACT TWO

Cheers as a carriage arrives with the KING. Sitting opposite him are CAVOUR and a FRENCH GENERAL.

Louder cheers for the next carriage in which MAZZINI sits. He acknowledges the crowd, nodding gravely. The cheers rise to offstage cries of 'Garibaldi si!' The KING's carriage exits.

An explosion of noise as GARIBALDI enters on foot – with JESSIE and GENERALS CRISPI and BIXIO. Limping, GARIBALDI waves his stick to the crowd. Hats are thrown in the air. JESSIE is pushed away but GARIBALDI rescues her.

TOWNSFOLK
Garibaldi for King! Garibaldi! Garibaldi to rule –
Garibaldi as Dictator – Garibaldi, si!

GARIBALDI lifts a hand for silence. Eventually there is a hush. He squints up at the balcony where the KING, CAVOUR, and the FRENCH GENERAL are now appearing, and looking down on him.

GARIBALDI
Friends – friends – what are you asking?

TOWNSFOLK
Garibaldi for King! Garibaldi!

GARIBALDI
You want me for King? What for?

TOWNSFOLK
For freedom – for Italy! For our country! For our Leader!

PEASANT
To make us rich!

MAN WITH CHILD
Every man a millionaire!

Cheers. Laughter. GARIBALDI waits for silence.

> GARIBALDI
> That's what you want of me? You want Giuseppe
> Garibaldi to make you rich?

Some calls of 'yes.' They die away.

> GARIBALDI
> Rich! *(Laughs.)* I can't even make myself rich! But
> I'll tell you this, lads. We're none of us going to get
> rich with the Austrians and the French here thieving
> everything.

> TOWNSFOLK
> Down with the Austrians! Down with the French! Go
> home, Frenchmen! Froggies go home!

The FRENCH GENERAL is outraged. He protests to CAVOUR and, as the noise rises, he leans over the balcony, and shakes his fist.

GARIBALDI lifts his stick for silence. The crowd goes still.

> GARIBALDI
> Why is the foreigner here? What for, if not to exploit?
> At most, he offers the bread of charity. My friends,
> the taste of that bread is bitter!

Shouts. Fists are raised against the balcony. CAVOUR whispers to the KING, then ushers the KING and the FRENCH GENERAL from the balcony.
Cheers.
All sing 'Chorus of the Hebrew Slaves' from the opera Nabucco by Giuseppe Verdi.

> Va', pensiero, sull'ali dorate;
> Va, ti posa sui clivi, sui colli,
> ove olezzano tepide e molli
> l'aure dolci del suolo natal!

> Del Giordano le rive saluta,
> di Sionne le torri atterrate ...
> Oh mia Patria sì bella e perduta!
> O membranza sì cara e fatal!
> Arpa d'or dei fatidici vati,
> perché muta dal salice pendi?
> Le memorie nel petto raccendi,
> ci favella del tempo che fu!
> O simile di Solima ai fati,
> traggi un suono di crudo lamento;
> o t'ispiri il Signore un concento
> che ne infonda al patire virtù!

Fade out.

ACT TWO – SCENE FOUR

The Royal Court. A stateroom. A sunny day.

CAVOUR and the KING. CAVOUR paces back and forth, quickly and nervously. The KING waves a hand.

KING
You're making me giddy

CAVOUR
He must be stopped – now!

KING
What do you suggest?

CAVOUR stops pacing. They regard each other for a moment. Then both shake their heads.

CAVOUR
They'd kill us.

KING

> (*Looking at CAVOUR behind CAVOUR'S back*)

Ye-es.

CAVOUR

The French have made it clear. They want him out of Rome.

KING

How?

CAVOUR

To remove Austria from this peninsular, we need France and its disciplined troops – not a band of buccaneers.

KING

It won't be easy. What am I to say?

They pace, crossing each other.

KING

If we sent his Generals with him –

CAVOUR

No, no, no.

They stop, look at each other.

KING

You're right. Divide and rule.

They shake their heads and resume pacing.

CAVOUR

What if we make him an ambassador?
A representative of the king of Italy?

ACT TWO

KING

Of Italy. Yes. *(He sits, then shakes his head)* No, it won't work.

CAVOUR

Why not?

KING

He'll see through you.

CAVOUR

I shall invoke his patriotism.

KING

Hm. If he were fool enough to agree, they'll treat him as a conqueror.

CAVOUR

What of it? He'll be out of the way, and we can stabilise the situation here by deploying French troops against the Austrians.

KING

Hmm. What about Garibaldi's men?

CAVOUR

We'll send them somewhere. Some...beach.

KING

(Rising)

Very well. See what you can do. I need to see my tailor.

CAVOUR

(Bows)

Majesty.

The KING goes. CAVOUR beckons for ASTI who enters.

CAVOUR

Where is he?

ASTI shrugs diffidently.

ASTI

One of the chambermaids is a beauty.

CAVOUR

Goddam it – ah, General!

As GARIBALDI erupts into the room tying his neckerchief.

GARIBALDI

Fine weather we're having.

CAVOUR

Gorgeous. Have a seat, General. How's the leg?

GARIBALDI

I seem to manage.

CAVOUR

Bravo. Have a seat.

He nods to ASTI, who goes. GARIBALDI sits.

CAVOUR

We have a proposition – a request. Of the most serious – the most exalted – nature to put to you.

GARIBALDI

Exalted?

CAVOUR

It is the King's wish that you visit the courts of Europe. As champion of the new Italy.

GARIBALDI

Me?

ACT TWO

CAVOUR

Who more appropriate? Our beloved hero – the creator of Italy.

GARIBALDI

You want me – as a politician?

CAVOUR

May I remind you that politics begin where the bayonet leaves off.

GARIBALDI

And where the lying begins.

CAVOUR

Signor General, who do you think I am? Some diplomat? Thinking twice before saying nothing? I am His Majesty's Minister. And on behalf of the State, and the King, I am entitled – nay, empowered, emboldened, and instructed to lie!

GARIBALDI

Not me.

CAVOUR

Have you never told a lie? Never knelt by a dying soldier, swearing he would be well by morning? Promised reinforcements, knowing they're not coming? Told your mistress you're going to return to her?

GARIBALDI

The small falsehoods of kindness.

CAVOUR

Ah, your lies are virtuous, mine are not!

GARIBALDI

Because you, sir, are a politician, and those who enter politics do so for power and profit.

CAVOUR

You believe there is not one man who seeks simply to be of service to his country?

GARIBALDI

If such a man exists I've never met him.

CAVOUR

By God, you condemn us all as rogues!

GARIBALDI

As you do – being one yourself.

CAVOUR

(Smiles)

I gather you don't like me, General.

GARIBALDI

No more than you like yourself.

For the first time, CAVOUR is out of face.

CAVOUR

I have never given thought to the matter.

GARIBALDI

A man who liked himself would not be eating himself into apoplexy, Count Cavour.

CAVOUR

Uh?

GARIBALDI

Do you wish to serve the people of Italy so little that you wish yourself so visibly out of life?

ACT TWO

CAVOUR
(Cold)
I beg your pardon?

GARIBALDI
So, you can be touched off! As you see, I am not a gentleman, but I apologise. I shouldn't have mentioned your belly. So, you want me out of Italy?

CAVOUR
Good Heavens, no! But we need a voice. A spokesman for the Republic. For Italy. General, you are Italy's finest weapon! A man of courage – of the people...

GARIBALDI
I'm no orator...

CAVOUR
You're a compelling man, Giuseppe.
Brave – handsome...

GARIBALDI
(Modest protest)
Wounded, arthritic...

CAVOUR
The ladies of Rome worship you.

GARIBALDI
They won't leave me alone! How am I supposed to see to them all... it's impossible! They've had half the hair on my head for keepsakes!

CAVOUR
Then what do you say? A sabbatical. Travel, in comfort for once. A chance for your wounds to heal. (GARIBALDI *looks at him drily.*) By God, I need a man who will tell me the truth – give me

Europe's response ... not for my sake, for Italy. (*As GARIBALDI absently smooths his hair*). The King's barber is in the building. His tailor too.

A pause. Then GARIBALDI shakes his head.

GARIBALDI

No, no. No, no, no.

CAVOUR

(*Looks outside, sighs*)

A pity. If I were free I'd go myself. What I wouldn't give to see that green and pleasant land.

GARIBALDI

England? Aha – the little Queen eh?

CAVOUR

(*Turns to face him*)

Oh no. Tennyson. Alfred, Lord Tennyson.

He quotes from 'In Memoriam,' blissfully savouring the words.

CAVOUR

Nor, what may count itself as blest,
The heart that never plighted troth
But stagnates in the weeds of sloth,
Nor any want-begotten rest.

GARIBALDI looks surprised. Then responds with the next verse.

GARIBALDI

I hold it true, whate'er befall,
I feel it when I sorrow most,
'Tis better to have loved and lost
Than never to have loved at all.

CAVOUR

Ohh! to sit at the feet of Tennyson ...

ACT TWO

GARIBALDI rises. They gaze at each other and embrace. Then they leave, heads together, CAVOUR helping GARIBALDI out. He returns at once with ASTI.

CAVOUR

Asti, am I putting on weight?

ASTI

No, Excellency.

CAVOUR

I thought not. I mustn't get fat, it will make me look ridiculous. Prepare the General's itinerary for a European tour.

ASTI

You mean you've persuaded him?

CAVOUR shrugs modestly.

ASTI

How?

CAVOUR

One thing about soldiers I can never understand. They read poetry. God knows why.

ASTI

Poetry?

Puzzled, he follows CAVOUR offstage.

Fade to black.

ACT TWO – SCENE FIVE

England. A Victorian sitting-room.

AGNES, the maid, scurries across the stage, ribbons flying.

Women's voices, raised, then silence.

MR ATTRILL, the gardener, pokes his head round the door, enters with a large trug of fresh flowers and grunts, displeased at finding no-one there. He turns to go as LADY TENNYSON enters at the run.

LADY TENNYSON

Go away ... oh I'm sorry it's you Attrill ... tell Agnes to look at the beef and to bring the purple jug. On second thoughts, the fluted vase – no, the jug and the green boat – what do you think?

ATTRILL's expression is grim.

LADY TENNYSON

Oh, all right, the flute – but not the small flute, the big flute ... and the bowl with the snakes from the lower landing windowsill. Go on, you silly man! *(Calls, off)* Baste the beef, Agnes! Baste the beef!

ATTRILL stumps off very slowly. LADY TENNYSON swerves away dangerously, fielding a tall, hideous vase en route. She rips out the pampas grasses within – spins, uncertain – then throws them out of the window where they land on LORD TENNYSON, who mistakes the pampas grass for swooping birds.

TENNYSON

Ah! Sweet feathered fiends ... friends ... rejected by the skies ...

Repentant puffballs, pansied o'er the vale ...

LADY TENNYSON begins to ram flowers into the vase. as AGNES, ATTRILL and the GARDENER'S BOY appear, all laden with vases. AGNES fills vases swiftly. LADY TENNYSON dumps an armful of

ACT TWO

flowers on ATTRILL. The GARDENER'S BOY fields a vase as she knocks it

LADY TENNYSON

Quick! The diligence will be at the door any moment... ah!

A screech as she reads the watch pinned to her bosom.

LADY TENNYSON

No, not like that, you toad, oh I'm sorry, Attrill, I didn't mean to call you a toad ... please! *(As he turns to go, affronted)* If we could have just a few more of your lovely blooms, for the what-not?

ATTRILL

You can 'ave 'ollysocks, nastyursinums and montybritches, mum.

He goes, with fearsome dignity, clouting the GARDENER'S BOY, who is holding a delphinium. Meanwhile, despite LADY TENNYSON's manic gyrations, AGNES fills vases and clears up behind her mistress as TENNYSON appears in a green velvet jacket, check trousers and brown wide-awake hat. He enters and crosses slowly from up right to up left, his languid, pensive movements in sharp contrast to those of the flower arrangers. The moment that he disappears, the doorbell sounds with an elongated, melancholy sound.

The flower arrangers stop dead, rigid with alarm. LADY TENNYSON gives a little shriek, takes off her apron, and swoops wildly towards the looking glass to tidy her hair. TENNYSON reappears.

TENNYSON

Did someone toll? *(His WIFE nods, too nervous to speak.)* Alas, it is the chiming of the bell, that from the spire doth lend its awful moan ...

LADY TENNYSON looks out of the window, leaning out dangerously, looking around a corner. She turns from the window, eyes wide.

LADY TENNYSON

It is he.

TENNYSON seems not to hear her.

TENNYSON

Too sullied now within the eroding heart ...

LADY TENNYSON

Our Italian guest has arrived. Alfred?

TENNYSON stands, remote. And then slowly begins to cry.

LADY TENNYSON
(Briskly)

Not now, dearest, Signor Garibaldi is here ... cry later.

GARIBALDI erupts into the room. At the same moment, ATTRILL, the gardener, enters separately, hidden behind huge flowers.

GARIBALDI

Bravo – bravo! *(He grasps the flowers to his bosom, sniffs deeply)* Ah! *(Lifts flowers high)* Poems from the poet!

He embraces ATTRILL fervently.

ATTRILL

Mind my foot!

GARIBALDI

Never shall it be said that the English have not the romantic heart! We Latins understand poetry ... I come in adoration.

ACT TWO

He kneels at ATTRILL's feet. ATTRILL, grumbling, picks up the blooms that have fallen on the floor and goes off with them, muttering to himself.

> TENNYSON
> *(Wistful)*
> I am Alfred Tennyson.

GARIBALDI, startled, embraces him – a long warm embrace.

> GARIBALDI
> Who was this man?

> TENNYSON
> The gardener.

> GARIBALDI
> Impostor! Signora!

He takes LADY TENNYSON's hand, imprints it with a gentle kiss, smiling up at her tenderly.

> GARIBALDI
> I bathe in your eyes ... the eyes of a wounded, thin sparrow ... and this one *(slapping AGNES on the behind)* ... the eyes of a big fat pigeon. *(Offending both women.)* To the kitchen! Quick, quick we are very hungry ...

AGNES disappears. To LADY TENNYSON, taking her arm.

> GARIBALDI
> And what surprise have you for a hungry hero? Something unusual? Some little ...bird? To be scrunched up between the teeth, ah? *(She begins to melt in his eyes.)* So long as is not thee rozbif ... all the time I am eating the rozbif – rozbif, rozbif, sitting

here and pushing up the liver. (*Holds stomach.*) Like
this – oump, oump!

LADY TENNYSON, aghast, rushes off.

>TENNYSON
>
>A glass of wine, Signor Garibaldi?

>GARIBALDI
>
>Ah!

He joins TENNYSON at a small round table in the window. TENNYSON pours from a decanter.

>TENNYSON
>
>It's Italian. (*GARIBALDI takes a drink*) From the
>local grocer. To your liking?

GARIBALDI makes a strangled sound. TENNYSON takes a sip.

GARIBALDI watches his face. TENNYSON looks over his glass.

>TENNYSON
>
>Adder's piss.

And the two men laugh, and are easy with each other.

>GARIBALDI
>
>My friend – to drink Italian wine you must come to
>Italy.

>TENNYSON
>
>I should like that very much. (*But he sighs, and looks
>out of the window.*)

>GARIBALDI
>
>Why not? Safe passage assured in Italy now. Thanks
>to me.

ACT TWO

> TENNYSON
> *(Smiles)*

Yes.

> GARIBALDI

You travel light ... a notebook or two, eh? Not like shifting an army ... victuals ... reserves ...

> TENNYSON

No.

> GARIBALDI

I – Giuseppe Garibaldi – invite you, though I don't live in a palace such as this – *(as TENNYSON demurs)* – I am a simple man. *(As TENNYSON shakes his head)* Why not? Bring your woman – or not, as you please. All the same to me, plenty of girls there ... boys ...

> TENNYSON
> *(Murmurs)*

Signor Garibaldi.

> GARIBALDI

Sorry, forgot you were English ... What do you say? Do you know Italy? The Po valley – Verona, Vicenza, Venezia?

> TENNYSON
> *(Sighs)*

I wish it were possible.

> GARIBALDI

Your family? Your health?

> TENNYSON

Not as such. *(But he looks about to cry.)*

GARIBALDI
(Assesses him keenly)

Ah, I see.

He bangs the table, making TENNYSON tremble.

GARIBALDI

Sunshine and Bacchus ... sunshine and Bacchus will melt the melancholy from every orifice in your body. I guarantee, Signor Poet.

TENNYSON

Yes. I daresay.

He lifts the decanter to GARIBALDI. GARIBALDI instinctively refuses, then shrugs, and accedes. TENNYSON refills his glass. They both drink. TENNYSON cheers up a bit with the wine.

TENNYSON

Good of you to make the journey.

GARIBALDI

The least I could do!

TENNYSON

It's out of your way. To be frank, I am surprised that a man of action ... the man who has united Italy –

GARIBALDI

I have!

TENNYSON

I am amazed and curious that you should want to journey to the Isle of Wight to meet a poet.

GARIBALDI

Then you are less of a poet than I took you for!

TENNYSON

And you are even more of a man.

ACT TWO

They drink in unhurried amicability. TENNYSON studies GARIBALDI, who, aware of it, presents his profile nobly.

GARIBALDI

Well?

TENNYSON

You're a handsome fellow. And, I admit, something of a surprise.

GARIBALDI

Because I don't look like an organ grinder? What did you expect? No, tell me, tell me!

TENNYSON

(Mournfully)

Military idiocy.

GARIBALDI

I've met plenty of that. But I am a sailor, not a soldier. And I did not, as you say, take the king's shilling. Not a life I chose, slaughtering the sons of mothers. No, no, I fought by chance. I am alive by chance, though, by God ... *(He bangs the table again, causing TENNYSON more grief.)* ... I am the bravest man I know! Fear is a stranger to me. Can you explain that?

TENNYSON

No. I am frightened day and night – and have been for as long as I can remember.

GARIBALDI

Then you are the braver man. *(He grasps TENNYSON's hand fervently.)* May I call you by your name – your given name?

TENNYSON

I should be honoured.

GARIBALDI

No, no, no – *(he wrestles TENNYSON's hand in a moment of irritability.)* I am speaking seriously.

TENNYSON

(Looking into his eyes.)

Then I am affected that you wish to do so.

GARIBALDI

Alfred – I love you.

TENNYSON

And I you, Giuseppe. I shall worry for your safety.

GARIBALDI

No! Think of me and laugh at this silly man – this foreigner! Then I shall have brought you a fine gift!

He rises, refills their glasses. TENNYSON rises and they drink to each other.

TENNYSON

(Toasting GARIBALDI)

To the poet.

GARIBALDI

(Toasting TENNYSON)

To the soldier!

GARIBALDI clasps an arm around TENNYSON's shoulder.

GARIBALDI

Come, let us see what your beautiful wife has managed to find to replace the damned roast beef, heh?

He laughs. And, amazingly, slowly, TENNYSON starts to laugh. They exit, arms about each other.

Fade to black.

ACT TWO

ACT TWO - SCENE SIX

The Island of Caprera.

CAMPION is stretched out in the sun, reading. SIGNOR B approaches. CAMPION drops his hat over his face, and pretends to be asleep.

SIGNOR B
Ah, good morning, Signor, having a sleep? A lovely morning for it – no rain at all since it stopped.

He toddles off. GARIBALDI, offstage, singing. He enters, and finishes the song. CAMPION applauds, and helps him to sit. GARIBALDI indicates for him to pick up his notebook.

GARIBALDI
Where were we?

CAMPION
Lord Tennyson.

GARIBALDI
Ah – Tennyson! A great artist. I suggested shorter poems.

CAMPION
Did he mind?

GARIBALDI
Not in the least! A fine man – and a fine poet.

CAMPION
I agree.

GARIBALDI
No good in a skirmish of course.

He goes silent.

> CAMPION
> Do you mind? That it is all over – that part of your life?

> GARIBALDI
> No. (*Slight pause.*) Perhaps at night.

> CAMPION
> At night?

Fade to black.

ACT TWO – SCENE SEVEN

On the campaign. Night.

SOLDIER #1 and SOLDIER #2 bend over a cauldron. SOLDIER #1 sniffs, doubtful. SOLDIER #2 sniffs – also doubtful.

> SOLDIER #2
> I wouldn't say it smells bad.

They continue their cooking. SOLDIER # 3 pens a letter for a friend.

> SOLDIER #3
> How's this? 'Dear' – what's her name?

> SOLDIER #1
> Amalia.

> SOLDIER. #3
> (*Filling in her name*)
> 'Dear – Amalia. My love floats on the paper from me to you. I wish I was in your arms and not here with these stinking, cursing soldiers. We are hungry. We marched all night then fought the enemy. Alessandro is no more. Tell his mother. I send you the love of my

ACT TWO

body and my hands are upon you, Amalia, my only love. Forever, Paolo.'

SOLDIER #1

Thanks. Ah –

SOLDIER. #3

What? You want me to say some more?

SOLDIER #1

No – it's just – could you copy it out again – twice?

SOLDIER #3

Why?

SOLDIER #1

One for Letizia and one for Emilia-Maria.

GARIBALDI enters, cigar in mouth, slaps away a mosquito.

GARIBALDI

Ah, cooking – *(dips with the ladle)* – eels?

SOLDIER #1

We're not sure. General – *(points to his mate.)* His wife's had a boy!

GARIBALDI clasps the SOLDIER #2"s hand, and embraces him.

SOLDIER #2

We want to name him after you, General – Giuseppe Garibaldi Palermo.

GARIBALDI

Palermo?

SOLDIER #2

He – we made him there ...

> SOLDIER. #4
>> *(Rushes on)*
>
> General!
>
> SOLDIER #5
>> *(Rushes on)*
>
> There's a fence!
>
> SOLDIER #6
>> *(Breathless)*
>
> A lemon bush ...
>
> SOLDIER #7
>> *(Rushes on)*
>
> And a – and a – *(too breathless to speak.)*
>
> SOLDIER #5 & SOLDIER #6
>
> – an olive tree –
>
> SOLDIER #7
>
> – coming up the lane!
>
> GARIBALDI
>
> Snipers. Use the knife.

The SOLDIERS dodge off. Silence. Then a horrible cry, followed by a moan.

> GARIBALDI
>
> Good. Eat up, lads!

He goes, slapping away another mosquito. The other SOLDIERS return as the stew is ladled out.

Everyone falls to ravenously. And are promptly sick.

Fade to black.

ACT TWO

ACT TWO - SCENE EIGHT

The island of Caprera. Night.

We can see the moon and the sea. GARIBALDI and CAMPION.

FRANCESCA enters to take away their dirty plates.

>GARIBALDI
>
>*(Handing her his plate.)*

Very tasty, beloved.

She glares at them suspiciously and goes. GARIBALDI leans back, eyes closed. He sighs.

>CAMPION

A peaceful spot.

>GARIBALDI

Bare rock. Wind. Goats that eat every blade of grass.
Yet I am content.

>CAMPION

This is home – your home.

>GARIBALDI

Ah, home! The smell of the first air you breathe.
Orange leaves at the window, sand between your toes.
The back end of every dog in the village – all known,
recognised. A man must know who he is, Campion.
How else can we make our way in the world?
Brothers, sisters, aunts ... can't always like them of
course. A harsh father? A careless mother? Forgive
them! Learn from their mistakes. Never forget the
leaden eyes of the orphan, combing the world for his
mother, his own home.

CAMPION

Yet everywhere people are emigrating.

GARIBALDI

Emigration bleeds the best from where they are most needed – their native land! Poor devils, when they prosper, they're poor. Read their letters. Do they love their new country? Does it have their loyalty? Loyalty is where the heart is, believe me. That is something I'm in a position to know more than most, and I wish it were not so.

The lights go down. SOLDIERS lie across the front of the stage. The smoke of battle. Then the moans begin, at first softly. Cries of pain from wounded men.

SOLDIER #1

Oh, please – please ...

SOLDIER #2

Water ...

SOLDIER #3

Mother – I want my mother!

SOLDIER #4

Take me home!

SOLDIER #1

Oh, please – mama, mama ...

SOLDIER #2

Water ...

SOLDIER #4

I want to go home ...

ACT TWO

The scene is held on SOLDIERS crying, moaning, and calling out. Then lights down on the front of the stage. Lights up on GARIBALDI and CAMPION.

GARIBALDI

Believe me, Campion, when we lose our bearing we lose the sextant of ourselves.

CAMPION

General – truly – you should be King of Italy!

FRANCESCA

(Arriving, arms full)

Huh!

She pushes them aside, dumps things and goes. The SPY and SIGNOR B bring on a table, and arrange seating and decoration.

CAMPION

Hullo! Are we to have a celebration?

GARIBALDI

It's nothing. A birthday.

CAMPION

Of course! Yours! Of course!

GARIBALDI

Why the devil do women put such store by birthdays?

CAMPION

Perhaps to celebrate survival.

GARIBALDI and CAMPION are hustled out of the way as decorative lights come on, and the SOLDIERS rise to become GUESTS.

MUSIC. JESSIE and the MARQUESA arrive separately. Cheers, off. GARIBALDI enters, born aloft by BIXIO and others.

>   ALL
>
> A song, General – a song!

GARIBALDI sings 'Libiamo ne' Lieti Calici' from Verdi's La Traviata.

The others join in on the choruses.

>   GARIBALDI
>
> Libiamo ne' lieti calici
> che la bellezza infiora;
> e la fuggevol ora
> s'inebrii a volutta.
> Libiam ne' doci fremiti
> che suscita l'amore,
> poiche quell'occhio al core
> onnipotente va.
> Libiamo, amore, amor fra I calici
> piu caldi baci avra.
>
>   ALL
>
> Ah! Libiam, amor fra' calici
> piu caldi baci avra.
>
>   GARIBALDI
>
> Tra voi sapro divider
> il tempo mio giocondo
> tutto e follia nel mondo
> cio che non e piacer.
> Godiam, fugace e rapido
> e il gaudio dell'amore
> e un fior che nasce e muore,
> ne piu si puo goder.
> Godiam!
> C'invita un fervido
> accento lusinghier.

ACT TWO

ALL

Ah! Godiamo!
La tazza e il cantico
La note abbella e il riso,
in questo paradiso
ne scopra il nuovo di.

Applause.

The TWO LADIES sit either side of him, with JESSIE glaring at her rival.

GARIBALDI slips away from between them as FRANCESCA, bedecked, appears. He joins CAMPION.

GARIBALDI

Too many women.

CAMPION

You have always been popular with the women, have you not, General?

GARIBALDI

Campion, I never ask twice!

The GUESTS raise their glasses.

ALL

To the General! The General! To the saviour of Italy! To the bravest man alive! Garibaldi, si! Garibaldi, si! Garibaldi, si!

Calls for a speech. GARIBALDI demurs, but is helped to his feet.

GARIBALDI

My friends ...

GARIBALDI takes his stance – one leg forward – and lifts his glass.

GARIBALDI
(Quietly)

To Italy.

The GUESTS raise their glasses.

ALL

To Italy. To Italy!

Music stops.

GARIBALDI

I believe ... I truly believe a man should love his own land.

Sounds of agreement. The MARQUESA applauds. GARIBALDI lifts his glass once more.

GARIBALDI

To a free and united Italy!

Glasses are raised. Murmurs of "To Italy." GARIBALDI settles back with CAMPION.

GARIBALDI

And damnation to all empires. To be the slave of another is to remain a child. A green plum.

JESSIE and SIGNOR B talk, heads together. FRANCESCA refills the glasses of the GUESTS, as a cordial hostess

CAMPION

Can foreigners never bring benefit?

GARIBALDI

As citizens, yes. As invaders, no. The relationship, even when peaceful, is tainted.

ACT TWO

CAMPION

Perhaps if we all became citizens of the world, with less national patriotism, there would be fewer wars. Frontiers no longer threatening because no frontiers.

GARIBALDI

Where there are no frontiers men will create them.

CAMPION

Surely a man can live where he chooses in a free world. What does it matter where you lay your head so long as the mattress is soft, the water pure, the grazing good.

GARIBALDI

Grazing is for cattle. Do we step out of the shell complete, like alligators? No. We are the product of our parents and our place. Look at this country, Campion. Is it not worth loyalty – protection? The most beautiful country in the world! The best olives, the finest wines.

The most beautiful buildings, the finest art!

SIGNOR B

And vines produce grapes, and grapes produce wine. As for olives ...

GARIBALDI covers SIGNOR B's head with SIGNOR B's poncho.

JESSIE

General! The man was making a profound observation!

Food is brought on. A team of local BOYS and GIRLS perform a grave and simple dance, to drum and tabor.

GARIBALDI rises to applaud, and is helped back to his seat.

GARIBALDI

Hold my hand Francesca.

She holds his hand, revealing her adoration.

GARIBALDI

I can hardly speak for tears. There is the future of Italy – a free, united Italy!

MUSIC of the Slaves Chorus from Nabucco. Lights lower.

GUESTS wander away. FRANCESCA sleeps across GARIBALDI's lap. The MARQUESA fills their glasses. She bends to CAMPION.

MARQUESA

My brave Academic!

She walks away with a backward glance, gratifying CAMPION.

JESSIE and SIGNOR B embrace vigorously.

CAMPION

Such a blessed, simple spot.

GARIBALDI

What more should a man need? Water ...food ...a roof over his head ...

CAMPION

Gainful employment?

GARIBALDI

(*As CAMPION relights his cigar for him.*)
His birthright! The need to contribute. Without that: venomous and despairing hearts. A man needs ...
(*puffs at his cigar*) ... what a man needs – what he must be granted – is his right to be a man. Not a slave. Not a beast of burden – but a man.

ACT TWO

CAMPION

And how would you define a man, General?

GARIBALDI

With his wife, as head of the family – respected – and indispensable. With the right to work – to protect – and to love.

CAMPION

General, you are that man.

GARIBALDI

I am, sir. I am.

Lights lower.

MUSIC. The middle section of 'The Slaves Chorus' from Nabucco, by Verdi. Soft at first, rising to full for the last chorus.

Fade to black.

The End.

GARIBALDI, SI!

CAST BREAK-DOWN (DOUBLING).

1. GARIBALDI
2. WILLIAM CAMPION – PRINCE METTERNICH – ENGLISH PROFESSOR
3. SPY – KING VICTOR EMMANUEL II
4. SIGNOR B – CARDINAL – MR ATTRILL
5. SOLDIER #1 – ARTIST – CAPTAIN ASTI – SAILOR #1 – MAYOR
6. SOLDIER #2 – VALERI – SAILOR #2
7. SOLDIER #3 – MAZZINI
8. SOLDIER #4 – GENERAL FRANCESCO CRISPI – COUNT CAVOUR
9. SOLDIER #5 – CAPTAIN BARBONE – FRENCH GENERAL – ALFRED LORD TENNYSON
10. BOY SOLDIER – ANDREOTTI – BOY IN NAPLES – GARDENER'S BOY
11. FRANCESCA – WOMAN IN NAPLES – AGNES
12. SEAMSTRESS – JESSIE – WOMAN IN NAPLES #2
13. THE MARQUESA – WOMAN IN NAPLES #3 – LADY TENNYSON

ASMs:

1. SOLDIER #6 – CROWD MEMBER
2. SOLDIER #7 – CROWD MEMBER

THE TREAT

For Frances Barber

THE TREAT

The Treat was first performed at the Institute of Contemporary Art, London, on 10 February 1984, produced by Jonathan Gems, directed by Philip Davis, and designed by Stephen Meaha.

CAST

Francine	FRANCES BARBER
Berthe	JENNY GALLOWAY
Marie	TRACY BODEN
Raymond	TIM STERN
Max	TIMOTHY SPALL
Jacques	TIMOTHY SPALL
Richaud	ALEX NORTON
Henri	BILL GIDDLEY
Jean-Louis	JONATHAN GEMS
Vincent	PETER ATTARD
The Mayor	TIMOTHY SPALL
Other parts played by	BILL McALLISTER
	JOHN ASHFORD
	MICHAEL MORRIS
	JEREMY KING
	MICHAEL WHELAN
Costumes designed by	JO THOMPSON
Lighting by	IAN GUGAN
Music Supervisor	PAUL SAND
Assistant Director	MICHAEL WHELAN

A movie adaptation of THE TREAT, written and directed by Jonathan Gems, was released in 1999, presented by Cineville, starring Patrick Dempsey, Daniel Baldwin, Michael York, Alfred Molina, Julie Delpy, Georgina Cates, Pam Gidley, Vincent Perez, Yancy Butler, and Seymour Cassel as the Mayor.

REVIEWS

"Feminists will love Pam Gems's 'The Treat' at the ICA Theatre. Most male chauvinist pigs who can take time off from abusing their partners will also find it a bit of a wheeze.

But what about those who profess no particular militant tendency and occupy the middle ground? They will not be so amused because this play has an ugly allegorical sting in its tail.

Rather like Ms. Gems's earlier play, GUINEVERE, this study suggests that, in terms of our attitudes to women, we are still very much in the Dark Ages.

She has set this latest offering in a 1920s brothel in provincial France, where, sexually, anything goes – and usually for the benefit of the local well-to-do.

The three whores who decorate the decadent establishment are on constant call. Whenever a new client lurches through the heavy curtains, they disrobe, pout, and generally present themselves as purchasable sex objects.

They are controlled by an obnoxious and profiting pimp who bullies them mercilessly. The customers, for their part, are beastly to a man. They prod, demand, insult, abuse – and more. The author gives them no redeeming features; they are rotters through and through. A line-up of lusting monsters who possess no human feelings.

So, it's a tough and demanding life for a poor girl in this man's world, especially for Marie, the one with religious inclinations who eventually dies as a result of her maltreatment.

She it is who becomes the set-piece treat in the macabre final sequence when the local mayor with a penchant for necrophilia is unwittingly catered for ...

The three girls, Jenny Galloway, Frances Barber and

Tracy Boden take the eye, but then they would because they have the author all on their side. The exotic mood of the piece is nicely established by Stephen Meaha's attractive set. A compelling and often witty play."

KEITH NURSE.
Daily Telegraph. 18/2/1982

"PAM GEMS proved with Piaf that she is not the kind of dramatist to pull any punches, and her new play, 'The Treat,' at the ICA, is a painfully bruising experience – particularly if you happen to be a man.

Set in a provincial French brothel in the twenties, it offers a continuously disparaging view of the male sex. Throughout, men are depicted as worse than animals – perverse in their appetites, cruel in their approach, unredeemed by the faintest hint of good humour or human kindness.

Although I feel Ms. Gems's attitude is grotesquely unfair, her play is far more rewarding than the average piece of angry feminist propaganda.

At times, it treads perilously close to sentimentality but, more often, the author reveals a robust compassion for her ill-treated women and, by the end, this chilling account of whoring and pawing achieves the nightmarish comedy of Joe Orton at his best ...

There is much moving playing from Tracy Boden as the dying, hysterical prostitute Marie, well supported by Frances Barber and Jenny Galloway, as her more earthly colleagues. Timothy Spall contributes a terrifying gallery of boorish male clients, winning laughter even as he appalls."

CHARLES SPENCER.
Evening Standard 17/2/1982

THE TREAT

SCENE ONE

A brothel in France in the Early Twenties.

The space is low-lit, with an effect of sumptuous charm. There are fresh flowers, an ottoman and other seating, a dressing table, a Japanese screen with a silk shawl over it, and a mini-bar with drinks – brandy, wine, and champagne on ice.

THREE WOMEN are present wearing Louis-heeled pumps of the period, lacy chemises in pale colours, and kimonos. FRANCINE is buxom. MARIE-HELENE is pale, thin, and fair. BERTHE is small.

FRANCINE is taking the hard skin off her heels with a file.

                BERTHE
I don't believe in him. (*To FRANCINE*) Do you?

FRANCINE temporizes – glances at MARIE

                FRANCINE

We-ell ...

                BERTHE
                (*Sturdy.*)

I don't.

                MARIE
                (*Half whispering in fear.*)

Please ...!

                BERTHE

Well, I don't.

MARIE claps her hands over her ears.

MARIE

I shan't listen!

BERTHE

I don't!

FRANCINE
(To BERTHE)
She's frightened he'll hear you.

BERTHE

Well, he won't.

MARIE
(Mutters.)
How can you be sure?

BERTHE

He won't because he's not there.

FRANCINE continues taking the hard skin off her heels with her file.

BERTHE
(Calls)
Are you there? Speak up, I can't hear you! (*To MARIE with sweet reason.*) See? There's nobody there!

MARIE
(Sullen.)
There is.

BERTHE

There isn't.

MARIE

There is!

BERTHE

Prove it!

FRANCINE

Now shut up, the pair of you.

BERTHE

You see, she can't. (*To MARIE.*) You can't, can you?

MARIE moves apart.

FRANCINE

Leave her alone.

BERTHE

I didn't start it.

FRANCINE

You did.

BERTHE

I never! She did! She asked me if I believed in him.

FRANCINE

No, she asked me.

BERTHE

Well, anyway, I don't. (*Pause.*) Waste of time. (*Pause.*) Ridiculous.

Pause.

FRANCINE

(*To MARIE.*)

Want a toffee?

MARIE

No thanks.

Pause. Then MARIE bends, gasping.

FRANCINE

What is it?

MARIE

(*Doubles up.*)

Cramps.

BERTHE

Again?

MARIE

I've had them all day.

FRANCINE

Tell him!

BERTHE

No, don't. You'll put him in a bad temper.

MARIE

I can't seem to ...

She gasps – doubling up again. FRANCINE glances offstage to make sure they're not observed, then serves MARIE some wine.

FRANCINE

Here. Sip it slowly. (*Standing over her.*) I'll have a word with the old girl downstairs.

BERTHE

Take an aspirin.

MARIE

I've had eight already. My head's ringing.

Pause.

BERTHE

(*To FRANCINE*)

What are you doing?

FRANCINE

Watching this fly clean its legs. It's got lovely little legs. There it goes ... Ahh!

MARIE crosses to the sofa and sits, gingerly. She half-collapses, then lifts up her feet and lies on the sofa.

MARIE

Oh God. Thou dost love us. Thou lovest and seest us in this our earthly torment ...

Enter the boss –MONSIEUR RAYMOND – with a MAN. As they enter, the GIRLS are immediately "on."

RAYMOND

La Choix, Monsieur. Mes enfants ... Monsieur ...
'Max.'

The MAN smiles at RAYMOND's choice of pseudonym for him.

MAX

Delighted.

The GIRLS lift their skirts to expose their bodies. Front first, then they turn, together, to expose their rear. MONSIEUR MAX walks along the line, taking his time, inspecting them with shrewd attention.

He gestures.

RAYMOND

Tournez, mes enfants.

They turn to the front again.

RAYMOND

May I introduce, Monsieur Max, for your pleasure ...
Mademoiselle Francine – fresh from the buttercup
meadows of ... ah ... Normandy. Mademoiselle

Marie-Helene (*Sotto Voce*) from a good family,
Monsieur, tragic story ... Et la petite Berthe!

MAX

Yers. Pas de fausse mineur?

RAYMOND

La petite Berthe will oblige, Monsieur.

MAX

She's too old.

RAYMOND

Monsieur will be amazed, I assure you. Allons, la petite!

BERTHE goes. RAYMOND gestures for MONSIEUR MAX to sit.

FRANCINE offers him a box of cigars, and a box of cigarettes. He chooses a cigar. She offers her thigh. He rolls the cigar against it. FRANCINE cuts it for him. MARIE lights it.

RAYMOND
(*Indicates the drinks.*)

Un petit peu, Monsieur?

MAX

What have you got there, Raymond?

RAYMOND
(*Pouring.*)

Un vrai petit vin du pays. You won't be disappointed.

MAX

Oh, where's it from?

RAYMOND

From the ...ah ...Auvergne. My home!

MAX tastes it, savouring.

THE TREAT

RAYMOND

We have others in the cellar, if Monsieur ...

MAX

No, no. This will do.

RAYMOND

A man of discernment. I know the vineyard
personally. My brother ...

MAX

It'll do. It'll do.

FRANCINE sits on his lap, displaying her bosom. He assesses it
through his cigar smoke, then glances at MARIE, who tosses her
head.

MAX

Yers.

RAYMOND

Good to relax, Monsieur, after a hard day
at ... er ... affairs and all that.

MAX

Yers.

RAYMOND

You need it. Good for the constitution.

MAX

Ah.

RAYMOND

And the bowels.

MAX blows out smoke. Looks at MARIE, who looks at him coldly
over her shoulder. RAYMOND gestures expansively, refilling his
own glass.

RAYMOND

A small establishment, as you see. But of superior quality. We cater to the man of taste. The man of sophistication.

MAX

So I've been told. Where's your negress? I don't see your negress. Is she ...? (*He waves a hand to offstage.*)

RAYMOND

Alas, not at the moment, sir. Matter of supply and demand. We like to keep up with the fashion, but I have my clients' pockets to consider. We don't go in for stupidity here. Next month, perhaps.

MAX has been eyeing MARIE heavily.

MAX

You. Come here!

She approaches and, at a glare from RAYMOND, intensifies her haughty languor.

MAX

Come on, girl, let's see what you've got.

MARIE

(*Cold.*)

Monsieur decides?

MAX

(*Slaps her.*)

Don't give me your airs and graces. You're nothing but a common whore. What are you?

He slaps her again.

THE TREAT

MARIE
(Sulkily.)

A common whore.

MAX

Sir!

MARIE

Sir.

She drops her kimono seductively, with a cold and resentful air.

MAX

And don't you forget it.

RAYMOND

Good for you, Monsieur. She's a haughty bitch. Needs putting in her place. (*To MARIE.*) Never mind what you were!

MAX

No. Too scraggy.

He pushes FRANCINE off his knee and turns her, in appraisal.

MAX

Good haunches, I'll give you that. I like plenty of weight on the haunch. You can keep your featherweights. Bar the fausse mineurs, of course.

RAYMOND

Oh, absolutely. A childlike scantiness...for the man of taste. In a certain mood. (*Hiccups slightly into his glass.*) Makes a change.

MAX assesses FRANCINE, who turns indolently in his hands.

MAX

Yers. A bit thick in the waist – but good quality.

THE TREAT

RAYMOND

Monsieur can be confident of that, we offer only the best, hand-selected ... Aha, voici ... Voila! La Petite!

BERTHE enters as the fausse mineur. She is dressed as a child, in white muslin, a blue ribbon round her waist. Her hair hangs to her waist, and she wears a large blue bow of satin ribbon on top of her head. She has on ballet pumps and white stockings and carries a wide-brimmed straw hat decorated with flowers and more ribbons.

She curtseys shyly to MONSIEUR MAX.

FRANCINE

Ah!! Isn't she sweet!

MARIE is not such a good actress.

MARIE

Lovely!

RAYMOND

Monsieur?

MAX

Very good ... very good ... excellent! (*He bends over BERTHE.*) And what's your name, little girl?

BERTHE

(*Half-whispers, in a lisp.*)

Lisette, Monsieur.

MAX

Come along now, no need to be frightened.

He pats her cheek. BERTHE droops, and rubs a knuckled fist into her eye.

FRANCINE

She's shy ...

MARIE

Awww!

MAX

(Crouching to BERTHE's level.)

You are not frightened of me, are you, little girl?

FRANCINE

Don't be silly, Lisette, the big man's not going to hurt you.

She holds out a dish of bonbons. MONSIEUR MAX selects one with precision, and holds it out to BERTHE on the palm of his hand. She swishes. He unwraps it, tantalizing her, then pops it in her mouth.

BERTHE

Thank you, Thir.

She curtseys, sucking prettily.

MAX

Such a tiny little mouth! My poor darling. Never mind, Daddy will be very, very gentle. Now, come along. I've got a great big surprise for you.

BERTHE

(Jumping up and down.)

Ooh! Is it a pwesent?

MAX

Aha! You must wait and see. But I want you to promise me something.

BERTHE

Yes, Daddy.

MAX

You must promise me not to scream. You won't scream, will you?

BERTHE begins to hang back.

> MAX
>
> Daddy will kiss your tears away. Come on ... (*Holds out his hand.*) Now, I don't want my little girl to cry.

BERTHE trembles, pulling away from him.

> FRANCINE
>
> Now she is being naughty.

> MAX
>
> Come along.

> FRANCINE
>
> She needs her bottom smacked.

RAMOND nudges MARIE.

> MARIE
>
> A good spanking.

FRANCINE, a bit too quick, hands him a large wooden HAIRBRUSH. He frowns at her over-promptness.

> BERTHE
>
> (*Weeping.*)
>
> Please, Daddy ... Please say you won't hurt me!

MAX drags her off by the hand.

> MAX
>
> Are you going to be a good girl?

> BERTHE
>
> Please don't hurt me! Don't hurt me ...

They go. And the others switch off like a light.

RAYMOND exits separately, and returns with a LARGE WICKER BASKET full of underwear.

THE TREAT

RAYMOND

Here you are. Francine, you mend the stockings. You've got a finer stitch.

FRANCINE

Oh, come on, guvnor! I'm getting prick marks all over my hands.

RAYMOND

Shut your mouth. I'm not having you girls sitting about doing nothing. Make yourselves useful.

He goes. FRANCINE pulls a horrible face at his back and pokes out her tongue. MARIE giggles.

MARIE

He never stops.

FRANCINE

Yeah.

But they pick over the mending, and begin to sew.

MARIE

How's your tooth?

FRANCINE

Fell out – yesterday.

She indicates – lifting the side of her mouth with her finger.

MARIE

Oh good.

FRANCINE

I'm saving up. Have 'em all out. Get a proper set – really white.

MARIE

Yes, I think I'll do that too.

They sew.

MARIE

What worries me is she could go to hell.

FRANCINE

No, she won't. She won't do that. Never.

MARIE

It's a terrible sin!

FRANCINE

How do you mean?

MARIE

Francine! Look at poor St. Peter!

FRANCINE

Oh...ah...mmm.

MARIE

She's so careless!

FRANCINE

I know what you mean. (*She bites off a length of thread.*) Still, if you look at it her way... I mean, she's got a point.

MARIE

How?

FRANCINE

You can't prove it.

MARIE

What do you mean? God is! He's there!

FRANCINE

Yes, but you can't prove it.

MARIE

You can.

FRANCINE

How?

MARIE

It's in the Bible!

They sew. A pause. FRANCINE holds up a pair of knickers.

FRANCINE

Look at this. All ripped. Isn't worth mending.

MARIE

That was last night. Monsieur Emile.

FRANCINE

I'll sew a bit of lace over it. He can pull that off for a thrill. I should just catch it together. Then he won't rip the cambric, and get us told off.

They sew.

MARIE

If I could only put it across to her.

FRANCINE

(Mutters.)

Oh no! (*Aloud to MARIE*) Don't take any notice. She's just being idle. Ignore her.

MARIE

I worry.

FRANCINE

Worry about yourself.

MARIE

(*Quick.*)

Why? Has he said something?

FRANCINE

Course not. Marie, he's not going to turn you away. You're his favourite.

MARIE

That wouldn't stop him.

Loud, awful screaming from within. MARIE merely raises her voice to be heard over it – then modulates her voice when the screaming ceases.

MARIE

He's always going for me. Making threats. When he's not messing me about, he's trying to frighten the life out of me...

RAYMOND ushers in an ELDERLY MAN wearing dated evening clothes and a cloak-coat, and holding a POSY OF FLOWERS. MARIE's voice changes effortlessly into an upper-class purr, as she rises and extends her hand.

MARIE

Monsieur Henri, what a charming surprise! How sweet of you to call.

HENRI

Cherie... Ma cherie...

MARIE

(*Taking the flowers.*)

For me? How delightful. White roses. So kind.

HENRI

La Divine! Divine! Embrasse moi... embrasse moi...

He dives for her.

                        HENRI

Ooh, your lovely tits! Your beautiful squashy tits.
Squeeze, squeeze...

                        MARIE

Monsieur Henri!

She slaps him lightly with one of his gloves.

                        MARIE

Naughty boy! Naughty boy! Ow!

                        FRANCINE
                    (To draw him off.)

Wine, Monsieur Henri?

                        HENRI

Ah, La Francine! Now, now... no need to feel
neglected. You shall have a cuddle later on at the
Mayor's party. Now, you must all be on top form. No
slacking!

                        FRANCINE

Depend on us, cher Monsieur.

                        HENRI

We'll have some real fun, eh? But first I must have a
little nibble at my lovely girl here...before the others,
heh, heh! Oh! (*His eyes shine.*) By the way, Francine –
guess who's coming tonight?

                        FRANCINE

Ooh... Who?

                        HENRI

Go on, guess!

FRANCINE, with a grimace aside, mimes guessing.

FRANCINE

I give up! Monsieur Henri, you're a terrible tease!

Above his head, she and MARIE exchange a derisory glance.

HENRI

I am, I am, I know! You'll never guess. Not in a million years! Have a go!

FRANCINE

Rudolph Valentino?

HENRI

No-o ...

FRANCINE

Ah ... the Kaiser?

HENRI

(Tantalising.)

No-o ...

FRANCINE

I've got it! Charlie Chaplin!

HENRI jumps up and down with excitement.

HENRI

No!

FRANCINE

(Losing patience.)

Who then?

HENRI

Your favourite! Your favourite – you know!

FRANCINE

What? Who?

> HENRI
>
> Monsieur Guillaume! The bald one! With the ...

He gestures a large stomach.

> FRANCINE
>
> *(Mutters.)*
>
> Oh, Monsieur Enceinte.

MARIE giggles behind HENRI's back.

> FRANCINE
>
> *(Still muttering.)*
>
> Eight months if he's a day.

> HENRI
>
> *(Chuckling.)*
>
> The one who likes to ...

He mimes whipping – pointing his finger at FRANCINE in delight.

> FRANCINE
>
> Ooh, yes. Bravo!

> HENRI
>
> You'll give him a good stroke back tonight, eh? And me ... And me!

> FRANCINE
>
> I shall be very firm with you both. Very firm.

> HENRI
>
> Oooh!

She turns him towards MARIE – kissing him lightly on the top of the head. HENRI goes, hanging on to MARIE's breasts. He has left his cloak. FRANCINE goes through the pockets absently. A routine task. But she finds nothing of interest. She finds a letter – reads it – shakes her head dismissively as the boss enters.

RAYMOND

Anything?

FRANCINE

Nothing. (*Waves the letter.*) It's only from his sister.

She inspects the cloak.

FRANCINE

This is worth a bob or two.

RAYMOND

Mean old sod. I wouldn't mind putting a touch in.

FRANCINE

Yeah. Local man. Be worth his while to cough up.

RAYMOND

Not him. Too mean by half.

FRANCINE

Write a letter, anonymous. Threaten to split. Tell his family.

RAYMOND

There's only the wife and the old girls. What do they matter?

FRANCINE

Send Big Louis round. Give him a punch in the head.

RAYMOND

No-o. No, he's too well in.

FRANCINE

I still think he wouldn't want his wife to know what he gets up to.

RAYMOND

Don't be a bigger twerp than you are. You want to sit in church of a Sunday, watch him put ten francs on the plate, and her sitting beside him in darned stockings, and a coat so old it's gone green on the shoulders. Scandalous – bloody disgrace.

FRANCINE

(Dry.)

I shouldn't worry.

RAYMOND

Why?

FRANCINE

Well, what she don't get, you do, eh? ... Haha ...

He turns on her, glowering.

FRANCINE

(Quickly.)

I still think he'd like it kept dark, guvnor.

RAYMOND

What are you talking about? People knew he was never out of the whorehouse, he'd be strutting around the town like a rooster! No, it won't work. Not with that old sod.

FRANCINE

Pity though.

RAYMOND

Yeah.

FRANCINE

He must be well off.

RAYMOND

(*Disgruntled.*)

Yeah.

FRANCINE

There must be something he'd mind.

RAYMOND

Keep thinking.

He gestures for her to get on with sewing, and goes. She picks up the sewing, but drops it as soon as he's gone, mutinous. BERTHE passes through. FRANCINE looks about but can't think of anything to do, so picks up the sewing, and sings to herself, a country song, low and sweet. BERTHE returns in her chemise and wrap, and picks up a piece of mending.

BERTHE

Thank God for small mercies. We're on our own for a bit.

FRANCINE

She's all right.

BERTHE

She's potty. Barmy.

FRANCINE

Look, if it makes her feel better ...

BERTHE

Why should I believe a lot of rubbish? Just to please her?

FRANCINE

Talk about something else.

BERTHE

You can't. She keeps coming back to it! Start a little conversation about having your shoes mended, or Portuguese oysters, straight back to God again. She's getting worse. She's been on it for days this time.

FRAN

All I'm saying is, just nod your head and agree with her.

BERTHE

What for?

FRANCINE

Because I say so.

BERTHE

You're not the boss! Anyway, why should I be the one to shut up? Why don't you tell her to shut up?

FRANCINE

She's an orphan!

BERTHE

(*Mock sympathy.*)

Ahh! So what?

FRANCINE

You know she's ill.

BERTHE

So she says. (*Mutters to herself.*) Believe what she wants. I'm not stopping her. Why blame it all on me?

MARIE enters, crosses the stage, exits, returns, and then sits, tying her kimono.

FRANCINE

You were quick.

MARIE

He felt queer.

FRANCINE

Oh, good.

BERTHE
(To Marie.)
You look better. You got a bit more colour.

MARIE

Yes, I don't feel so faint.

She rises, and picks over the sewing.

FRANCINE
(Sewing swiftly and deftly.)
Roll on the party, eh?

MARIE
(Dismayed.)
Oh, I'd forgotten! I can't face it.

BERTHE

Think of the food!

FRANCINE

I asked the old girl. It's quenelles, game pie, duckling, salmon, fromage a la crème and fresh pineapple.

BERTHE
(To MARIE.)
You like quenelles. Easy on the guts.

FRANCINE

Remember that soufflé au liqueurs? My favourite. Except for cherries and petit Suisse. I really love cherries – well, I like all fruit.

BERTHE

Except plums. Make you squit. (*To MARIE.*) You feeling all right?

MARIE nods, with a smile.

FRANCINE

I still dream of those wild strawberries, at the Baron's farewell.

BERTHE

You made a real pig of yourself there.

FRANCINE

I did, I know! A marble bath full of wild strawberries, silver buckets of cream. Gaw, they know how to live!

BERTHE

Remember the quail, inside the capon, inside the turkey, inside the swan?

FRANCINE

And the log fires, as big as a forest. Ooh, the heat!

BERTHE

And all the fairy lights in the trees, and that Italian woman, singing. (*To MARIE.*) Haha, you burst out crying!

FRANCINE

You looked really lovely that night. Just like the Virgin.

BERTHE

(*Tart.*)

That was the idea.

MARIE

So many flowers. Roses...lilies...

BERTHE

And the beds. What about the beds! Imagine sleeping in them. You'd never wake up!

MARIE

(With a little smile.)

Sleeping beauty.

She smiles again awkwardly. The others puzzle over this.

FRANCINE

Dunno about that. I do know I nearly had an orgasm. Quite disgusted meself. It was those silky sheets. You felt, you know, looked after.

BERTHE

Nice presents. Coty perfume.

MARIE

Fans.

FRANCINE

Those little evening purses with the tassels.

BERTHE

And Suzanne found herself a patron.

FRANCINE

No, it's off.

BERTHE

Why?

MARIE

What happened?

BERTHE

What happened?

FRANCINE

Fell for a baby. The old biddy who saw to her made a mess of it. She ended up in hospital.

BERTHE

Oh, not the hospital!

FRANCINE

And they did their usual. Left an arm inside her. She had it two weeks later. She's been ever so ill...septic. Lucien says she looks like a bladder of lard. Lost all her looks.

MARIE

Oh God, please God...

BERTHE

Poor kid. Still, she'll be all right. Legs like that, she'll never want for work.

MARIE

(Fearful.)

Not if she's lost her looks.

FRANCINE

I'll put a word in for her with the boss.

BERTHE

(Quick.)

No, you won't.

FRAN

Why not?

MARIE looks from one to the other.

MARIA

Has he said anything? He's said something, hasn't he?

FRANCINE
No. I was just trying to do her a good turn!

MARIA
He was looking at that girl in the bakery.

BERTHE
Rubbish. Anyway, we're better off on our own. I never liked Suzanne. Very argumentative. What's more, if we did ask that mean sod for anything ...

RAYMOND enters with a GLOWERING MAN.

BERTHE
(Winningly.)

Bonsoir, Monsieur!

RAYMOND
Mes enfants, je vous présente ... Monsieur 'Jacques!'

JACQUES
(Bleak.)

What?

RAYMOND
(Quick.)

La Choix, Monsieur. La Choix!

The GIRLS go through their routine, as before. JACQUES regards them, sourly.

RAYMOND
Monsieur wishes my recommendation?

JACQUES
What?

RAYMOND

Perhaps Monsieur could advise me as to his tastes. Some preference. We are a speciality house here.

JACQUES indicates FRANCINE.

JACQUES

I'll take this one.

RAYMOND

Aha! Monsieur prefers Mademoiselle ...

JACQUES
(Cutting him off.)
No! I don't want to know her name!

FRANCINE, quick on the uptake, gets up.

FRANCINE
(Submissively.)

This way, M'sieur.

She hurries offstage followed by 'JACQUES.'

BERTHE
(To RAYMOND.)

What's the matter with him?

RAYMOND

Never mind.

BERTHE
(To MARIE.)

He's had a row with his wife.

MARIE

How d'you know?

BERTHE

See it in his eyes.

RAY

> *(Cuffs her about the head.)*

Keep your bloody trap shut and get on with your work.

He goes. Sounds of a beating next door.

FRANCINE

> *(Offstage.)*

Stop it! Stop it! Ow! Ah! No, don't! Ah!

BERTHE

What did I tell you!

MARIE tries to sew but her hands shake. She puts down the work.

BERTHE

You feeling bad again?

MARIE nods.

BERTHE

Perhaps it's something you ate. That liver?

MARIE

I haven't eaten anything. *(Almost crying.)* It's all the time now. It never stops!

BERTHE

You're gonna have to pull yourself together. Otherwise ...

MARIE

> *(Low.)*

I know.

BERTHE, restless, sits at the dressing table, does her heavy makeup and redoes her hair. MARIE sits, trying not to shake.

THE TREAT

> BERTHE
>
> *(At the mirror.)*

Look after yourself more. Look ahead. Make plans for yourself. I do. (*She redoes her mouth.*) I don't intend to be doing this for the rest of me life. No, you have to plot it out. Learn to get your own way.

> MARIE
>
> *(Sad.)*

How?

> BERTHE

Start on little things. Work your way up. That's what I did. (*Trying a Spanish comb in her hair.*) One time, I wouldn't say boo to a goose. My first guvnor knocked me about something horrible if I didn't do my quota. I was working in Marseille. I hate Marseille. Horrible place. There's worse things than being an orphan. Anyway, I think so.

She finishes her toilette.

> BERTHE

But I knew something would turn up. I used to say to meself, keep your eyes open, Berthe...and it did. I met this Spanish bloke.

> MARIE

What happened?

> BERTHE

Took me to the races. He had a good day. We were drunk as newts after – him worse than me. I was through his pockets and on the train to Paris same night. Bought meself a whole new wardrobe – silk panties, the lot. All I need now is some old fart to set

me up. With a bit of luck, he'll peg out from it – then
I'm laughing, see? Know what I'm gonna do?

MARIE

No, what?

BERTHE

Run a sweet shop. My name over the shop – best
quality bonbons, all special wrapped. I'm having
gold and mauve for the ribbons, shiny pink paper
wrappings, special boxes for Easter, Noel, and
weddings and christenings.

MARIE

It sounds lovely.

BERTHE

Yeah. I'll live over the shop – all by meself. With a
little Pomeranian dog and a couple of cats. Persian.
And, out the back. I'll have me own little orchard. A
vine or two. A little place to sit ... for morning coffee.
I've even thought of keeping chickens.

MARIE

(Eyes glowing at the thought.)

Oh Berthe!

BERTHE

Just stand up for yourself. Enter into it. After all,
it's a high- class establishment here. We get a good
clientele. I mean, they come here for what they can't
get at home, which wouldn't be decent. All good
backgrounds, you know.

MARIE

(Slight pause.)

I bleed all the time.

BERTHE

What did the doctor say?

MARIE

That I was fit to work. No infection.

BERTHE

Perhaps you got a fibroid. They grow big as grapefruit – you think you're expecting! Just when you're sure it must be twins the bloody thing explodes. Either that, or it strangles your tripes, or blocks off your bladder so's you can't widdle. You constipated?

MARIE

No, I get diarrhoea all the time. It's like water.

BERTHE

Oh, good.

MARIE

It gives me such terrible cramps.

BERTHE

Tell him!

MARIE

He says I'm complaining.

BERTHE

But you've gone all thin!

MARIE

Raymond likes me like that.

BERTHE

Well, get round the bugger. Come on, he'll be back in a minute to see what we've done.

THE TREAT

MARIE tries to sew but cannot. BERTHE bites the cotton thread on her own bit, and throws it to MARIE.

BERTHE
Here. If he says anything, you've done that bit.

She fishes in the basket, and hands another piece to MARIE.

BERTHE
Pick the ribbons out of that one. Come on. Look, if you don't keep your mind together, you'll go really ill.

MARIE picks the ribbons from a cambric nightgown.

FRANCINE emerges, holding her face. She stumbles through, and sits down heavily. RAYMOND enters with TWO YOUNG DRUNKS.

RAYMOND
La choix, Messieurs. La Choix! Who is it to be this week, Monsieur Paul? La Belle Marie-Helene. Our little BERTHE of the dazzling derriere ...

BOTH MEN indicate FRANCINE, one murmuring in RAYMOND's ear.

RAYMOND
Aha! The triple crown! An excellent choice! Our beautiful Francine will accommodate you. (*He smacks her thighs.*) Strong thighs, messieurs. Perfect for your purpose. To work, Francine!

FRANCINE rises with a big smile.

MONSIEUR PAUL
Yes, come on, Francine! See if we can't do better than last week. I brought you off, didn't I?

FRANCINE
You did, you did. You're a real sportsman!

MONSIEUR PAUL

Not many do that with a whore.

RAYMOND

No, indeed, sir!

YOUNG DRUNK

(Goosing her.)

Come on, Francine! You can sit on my face anytime.

FRANCINE takes the arm of MONSIEUR PAUL, and steers them both off.

MONSIEUR PAUL

(Going.)

She's a goer ... Francine!

RAYMOND

You'll get your money's worth with Francine, sirs.
Worth every penny.

YOUNG DRUNK

(Hard voice.)

Oh, we'll see to that all right, all right. Don't worry yourself, Monsieur Pimpo.

RAYMOND, furious, trips over the sewing basket, making BERTHE giggle. He turns – picking up a garment.

RAYMOND

(Ugly.)

What's this?

MARIE

We put a bit of lace on. To cover the tear.

RAYMOND

Who said you could do that? Who said you could do that?

MARIE
(Small.)

Nobody.

RAYMOND

Who d'you think I am, the Aga Khan? Get it off! I've told you ... Only for gentry! Wasting good lace like that. D'you think I'm made of money? Get it off!

MARIE

It's all torn.

RAYMOND

Cobble it together, you stupid tart!

MARIE

I'll unpick it carefully and use the same bit of cotton to darn it.

RAYMOND

That's all very well – do the job twice. That's still my time you've wasted, you bitch!

He stomps off, muttering to himself.

BERTHE

Ooh, blimey.

MARIE

I should have thought.

BERTHE

Bloody mending! We shouldn't be doing it. The old girl ought to do it. It ruins your hands.

MARIE

That's what Francine said.

BERTHE

She's right! I was in trouble the other day with Monsieur Bertrand. He said my finger was real rough. Mind you, piles the size he's got, he's going to find anything painful.

MARIE

I know. As soon as you push them in, they pop out again.

BERTHE

Silly old twat. (*She jerks her head at the door.*) And him.

MARIE smiles. She watches BERTHE sew. A thought occurs.

MARIE

Berthe.

BERTHE looks up.

MARIE

You must have believed when you were little.

BERTHE

(*Grimaces fearsomely.*)

Look, please!

MARIE

(*Low. Apologetic.*)

It's just that it's such a terrible sin.

BERTHE

That's my worry, innit?

MARIE

Don't you care?

BERTHE

I care that what goes on in here ... (*She taps her head*) ...is mine. One thing they can't take away from you.

MARIE

But it's all in the Bible!

BERTHE

What proof's that? Tell me milk comes from a cow's tit, you can take me in a field, and squirt the milk in me face. That's proof! Anyway, God didn't write the Bible.

MARIE

He did. Well, he got his prophets to do it.

BERTHE

That's what I'm saying. It was a lot of old ginks. Isaiah, Jeremiah ... Numbers.

MARIE

They must have got it from somewhere. Where did it all come from?

BERTHE

God knows.

MARIE

That's just what I'm saying!

Loud thumping and squawking from next door.

MARIE

It had to come from God in the first place. Where else? God's everywhere. Everything in the world comes from God.

BERTHE

Even misery?

MARIE

It's sent to try us. We should feel blessed to suffer. To carry the sins of the world. He loves us, Berthe. We are loved!

BERTHE

Oh yeah? Like the time I lost me brother – sicking his lungs out all over the bed. And my fucking stepmother – worrying about the sheets getting dirty. And losing my little girl?

MARIE

Perhaps God needed her . . . on His right hand.

BERTHE

Why bother sending her then – putting me through it? Three days in labour. Bloody spiteful if you ask me.

MARIE

Berthe, don't.

BERTHE

I don't see why I should be picked out for punishment. I'm not wicked. There's a lot worse than me.

MARIE

We're harlots.

BERTHE

I don't think that's so bad.

MARIE

Most people do. The Church does.

BERTHE

Then bollocks to the Church.

MARIE

Oh no! Stop! (*She covers her ears.*) I can't listen!

BERTHE

Oh, go on. It's only swearing. Oh, all right. I'll wash me mouth out with cold cream.

She picks up a pot of cream from the dressing table, and puts some into her mouth.

BERTHE

Ugh!

MARIE giggles.

BERTHE

Anyway, I don't know what you want to listen to the Church for. That's just a lot of old men. Half the world's women! There wouldn't be any men if it wasn't for us. They thought all this up – Church and all that. It's meanness. To keep us down because we're quicker'n they are. Bloody have to be.

MARIE

Oh Berthe, don't say such things. The Church is our only refuge, our ...

BERTHE

Bugger the Church. Listen, who's the most reg'lar client we got? Father Anton! And who was it made you eat a shit sandwich? The bloody Bishop!

Thumping and screams from offstage.

BERTHE

Don't tell me there's a God. Devil maybe. (*Nods at the offstage noises.*) She's going to have a sore arse.

MARIE

Oh, thank God it's not me!

RAYMOND enters, murmuring obsequiously to a tall, bony, well-dressed MAN with a nervous and careful manner. This LE COMTE. The girls stand up.

RAYMOND

La Choix!

LE COMTE points to MARIE, and whispers to RAYMOND.

RAYMOND gestures to MARIE. MARIE exits. LE COMTE sits, looking straight ahead. BERTHE picks up the box of cigars to offer him, but RAYMOND shakes his head.

RAYMOND

(*Clears his throat.*)

A... a glass of wine, Monsieur le Comte? Brandy perhaps?

LE COMTE shakes his head, quelling them both with a glance.

MARIE enters, dressed as a NUN, carrying whips and chains. She looks distraught.

BERTHE

(*To MARIE*)

Thought things were a bit quiet.

MARIE exits with LE COMTE. RAYMOND exits separately, and re-enters with a BEARDED MAN.

RAYMOND
If you prefer to wait, Monsieur ... Or I can offer you La Petite Berthe.

BEARDED MAN
Too small? Nothing else?

RAYMOND
A few moments, Monsieur.

BEARDED MAN
I haven't got time. How much if I don't mount her? I don't find her attractive.

They move upstage, conferring, and striking a bargain.

RAYMOND
Right ... All right. (*He nods. To BERTHE.*) Be quick about it. I haven't got all night.

The BEARDED MAN and BERTHE exit. Pause.

FRANCINE enters, looking the worse for wear. RAYMOND exits and bids farewell to the TWO YOUNG DRUNKS, who are offstage.

RAYMOND
(*Offstage.*)
Au 'voir, messieurs, au 'voir. Come and see us soon. Always glad to welcome real sportsmen! Aha! Ha ha ha!

FRANCINE goes to the dressing table to repair her face. RAYMOND enters with MONSIEUR VINCENT, a heavily-built man in his sixties.

RAYMOND
Et voici La Belle Francine! Waiting to enjoy your company, Monsieur Vincent!

VINCENT

Francine! (*He embraces her.*) How are you, my dear? Plump as ever?

FRANCINE

Monsieur Vincent...

As they exit together...

VINCENT

I thought we might try a new variation this week. Have you got the little book?

FRANCINE

Of course.

They exit. BERTHE enters, crosses, and exits. Pause. BERTHE returns, sits, grabs an apple, but has no time to take a bite. RAYMOND ushers in JEAN-LOUIS, a young man.

BERTHE

(*Mutters.*)

God Almighty.

She rises, smiling.

RAYMOND

(*Indicating BERTHE.*)

Voila, Jean-Louis... La petite soeur de Monsieur.

BERTHE curtseys.

JEAN-LOUIS

Sho don't much look like our Paulette.

RAYMOND

She will, my dear young man. She will! Describe your sister, Monsieur.

JEAN-LOUIS
(*Sulky.*)
She's got long hair. And she's very shy.

BERTHE lets down her hair, and turns away, shyly.

JEAN-LOUIS
And she's got a smile like Saint Bernadette.

BERTHE smiles at him.

RAYMOND
(*Reverently.*)
Kneel, cher Monsieur ... Kneel.

The YOUNG MAN, mesmerised, kneels. BERTHE approaches, and puts a hand on his head. He groans and begins to pant.

BERTHE gives RAYMOND a quick look, then takes the YOUNG MAN's hand, and leads him off. MARIE enters, weeping quietly.

RAYMOND
What's the matter with you?

She displays her back, then her chest. She is covered in hot, red weals. And there are marks on her throat.

MARIE
He's getting worse! He'll kill me next time. You'll have to stop him, Raymond!

RAYMOND
(*Irritable.*)
How can I?

MARIE
Don't let him in!

RAYMOND
You know who he is. I can't do that!

MARIE

But I swear he'll ...

RAYMOND

I can't afford to upset the gentry. You'll have to take your chance.

MARIE

Raymond, please ...!

For a moment, he wavers.

RAYMOND

(In a temper.)

Now, don't start!

He goes.

FRANCINE enters, crosses the stage, and exits. She re-enters and sits.

FRANCINE

(Tired.)

Just old Vincent. All talk. Hullo, what's up?

MARIE shows FRANCINE her back.

FRANCINE

Oh, my God! No. That's too much.

MARIE

He'll kill me, Francine – next time, or the time after. I can see it in his eyes.

FRANCINE

What did the guvnor say?

MARIE

He said there's nothing he can do.

FRANCINE mutters under her breath, turns to the dressing table, and sponges her face, then attends to MARIE's wounds.

FRANCINE

He's scared to upset him. Wouldn't be the first time either. Turn around.

MARIE

What do you mean?

FRANCINE

Remember Esmeralda?

MARIE

The one who went to Italy with a lion-tamer?

FRANCINE

His idea of a joke.

She puts her hands round her own neck, and makes a choking sound.

FRANCINE

And one of the maids on the estate. They hushed it up. Said she tripped and fell down a well.

RAYMOND enters with a BUSINESSMAN.

RAYMOND

As you say, Monsieur.

BUSINESSMAN

At least she's got a good bum on her.

He grabs a buttock.

RAYMOND

Indeed, Monsieur.

FRANCINE and the BUSINESSMAN go.

RAYMOND

Vulgar bugger. I hate that sort of talk. Here, you'd better have this.

He gives MARIE a brandy.

A MAN in his sixties, formally dressed, enters.

RAYMOND

Monsieur Richaud! Entrez, my dear Monsieur Richaud. Marie-Helene! It's our old friend Monsieur Richaud. Oho! A grand occasion I see!

MARIE gives RICHAUD a languid hand. He kisses it gallantly.

MARIE

You're very welcome, Monsieur Richaud. Pray be seated.

RICHAUD

I can't stop, old thing.

RAYMOND gives him a vast balloon of brandy.

RICHAUD

Ah, thanks. (*He knocks it back with relish.*) Reception's in full swing up there!

RAYMOND

Oh, of course! Your daughter's wedding! Congratulations. A lovely day for it ... And you didn't forget us ...

RICHAUD

Just thought I'd drop in for a pick-me-up.

He gives RAYMOND a small box.

RICHAUD

A bit of cake for the girls.

RAYMOND

Ah! Marie-Helene – think of that! Oh, they will be pleased! Well, you know women!

RICHAUD

I do, I do. I should think I do. Five daughters!

RAYMOND

Mention the word wedding to my girls...Oh, they all pipe their eye!

He begins to refill RICHAUD's glass.

RAYMOND

To the young couple. May they have every happiness and prosperity... No, no, wait... This calls for something special.

He opens the champagne, and almost gives some to MARIE, then remembers who she is.

RAYMOND

So, reception's going well, eh?

RICHAUD

Costing a fortune. I can't bear to look. No, they're all dancing away there. Five-piece band. All the young ushers touching up the bridesmaids. Beautiful sight. Not a plain face among 'em. Ah!

RAYMOND

We're always here, old friend.

RICHAUD

I will say, she looks a treat, my little Anne. In her white dress. Fit to eat.

He and RICHAUD drink.

RAYMOND

A lovely girl. (*Pats RICHAUD on the knee.*) I tell you what. I've had an idea! Why don't we dress up Marie-Helene here as the bride? To celebrate the occasion!

RICHAUD

Oh, I wouldn't put you to the bother.

RAYMOND

Not a bit of it! The least we can do for a man who's losing his prettiest daughter – not that they aren't all good-looking ... Lovely girls. Off you go, Marie-Helene ... And the best dress. The one the Countess gave us. You know the one, my dear. With the real Brussels lace.

MARIE goes.

RAYMOND

Marvellous girl. Comes from a very good family, you know. Ah! All these lovely girls ...

RICHAUD

Yes. It's a very strange feeling. One minute they're sitting on your lap, asking for bonbons. The next, some chap's wanting to bounce about on top of them. Makes you think, Raymond. Makes you think.

Pause. They drink, reflectively.

RAYMOND

(*Discreetly.*)

Good arrangements?

RICHAUD

Can't complain.

RAYMOND

Ooh! She's marrying into a fine family, I hear. Building supplies, was it?

RICHAUD

And sanitary fittings.

RAYMOND

She won't go wrong there.

RICHAUD

Well, the wife saw to it all. She doesn't stand for any nonsense.

RAYMOND

A good match, eh?

RICHAUD

Oh yes. No, no ...she'll buckle down. They need an older man. Once she's had a couple of children ...by the time she's twenty, she'll have too much to think about ...

MARIE enters, dressed as a bride. She sways slightly, recovers, and smiles.

RICHAUD

Aha! Oh, my dear girl! Oh, what a picture! Bravo! You've done me proud, old friend.

Blows his nose in a large handkerchief, and breaks down.

RICHAUD

It's not every day a man loses his daughter ...

RAYMOND

And there's nothing wrong with a manly tear about it. You're a man of sentiment, sir. Nothing wrong with that, eh? Tell you what. Kiss the bride. Come. I now

pronounce you man and wife. Back with the veil, my
dear. You're a married woman now. She's all yours,
my friend – to have and to hold, eh? Look at her lovely
lips. They're trembling for it. She can't wait for your
hand on her ... It's what they're made for, friend. It's
what they're made for ...

>   RICHAUD
>
>   *(Groans.)*

Come here.

He kisses MARIE greedily.

>   RICHAUD
>
>   *(To RAYMOND)*
>
>   I shan't forget this, my dear fellow. I shan't forget
>   this. A day to remember!

He lifts MARIE in his arms and staggers off with her.

BERTHE enters.

>   BERTHE
>
>   I'm having trouble with Jean-Louis.

>   RAYMOND
>
>   What sort of trouble?

>   BERTHE
>
>   He's crouched down in the corner, crying. I can't get
>   him to move.

>   RAYMOND
>
>   Didn't he get off?

>   BERTHE
>
>   You kidding? I can't hardly stand up. I think he's
>   done me an injury.

RAYMOND

Let's have a look.

He pulls open the waist band of her dress and looks down.

RAYMOND

It's not too bad.

BERTHE

Can I stop work?

He cuffs her.

RAYMOND

You'll pack up when I tell you, and not before. Get washed.

BERTHE

What about the kid?

RAYMOND

I'll see to him.

BERTHE

Well, be careful.

RAYMOND takes a small bottle from his pocket, and gives her two tablets.

RAYMOND

Here ... You'd better have these.

BERTHE

Thanks, boss. You're a treat!

RAYMOND

Don't tell the others. And don't say I don't look after you!

They exit separately. FRANCINE appears, crosses the stage, and exits.

Pause. She returns, sits, and begins to doze. BERTHE appears, hobbling.

>   FRANCINE
>   *(Sleepy.)*
> What's up?
>
>   BERTHE
> Lunatic. Pain's just coming through.
>
>   FRANCINE
> Guvnor give you anything?
>
>   BERTHE
> Yeah.

FRANCINE gives her a sharp look. If tablets have been dispensed, the injury is real.

>   FRANCINE
> Put your legs above your head.

RAYMOND enters.

>   RAYMOND
> Messieurs ... La Choix!

TWO SOLDIERS follow him on.

>   FIRST SOLDIER
>   *(To SECOND SOLDIER)*
> Turn and turn about?
>
>   SECOND SOLDIER
> I'll take the littl'un first. Want a good poke, littl'un?

BERTHE smiles cheekily.

>   BERTHE
> You and who else?

The SECOND SOLDIER gooses her.

> BERTHE

Whoops!

> FIRST SOLDIER
> (*To FRANCINE.*)

Right. It's you and me, lovely. Look lively. We ain't got all night.

He whacks her bottom. She jerks forward.

> FIRST SOLDIER

That's better.

FRANCINE manages a grin.

> FIRST SOLDIER

We're here for a bit of fun, not for the knitting.
(*To RAYMOND.*) How much for sodomy?

> RAYMOND

Twenty, Monsieur.

> FIRST SOLDIER

Mmm, a bit steep. Thirty for the two?

> RAYMOND

Thirty-five.

> FIRST SOLDIER

Done. (*To BERTHE.*) That'll take the smile off your face, Titch.

> SECOND SOLDIER

Yeah!

> RAYMOND

My girls will accommodate you, sir – never fear.

SECOND SOLDIER

Been there, have you?

RAYMOND

Monsieur?

FIRST SOLDIER

Right. No cocking about. Here we go. Lead the way.
Fuck, fuck ... fuck, fuck, fuck ...

He marches.

SECOND SOLDIER

Girls were made to poke and suck!

The SOLDIERS laugh loudly as they go.

RAYMOND helps himself to champagne. He sits, sipping the champagne. MARIE enters, the wedding dress over her arm. Her white satin petticoat is ripped.

RAYMOND

All right?

MARIE

He gave me ten francs.

He puts out his hand, and pockets the money. MARIE exits, then returns in her kimono, carrying the wedding dress.

MARIE

The train needs mending, and the underskirt.

He looks at the damage.

RAYMOND

Dirty bastard.

MARIE

(Turning the dress over.)

I'd better see to it.

RAYMOND

No, come here.

MARIE

Oh Raymond, not now.

RAYMOND

Just a quick one. Come on.

She joins him. He starts caressing and kissing her. Then, he gets up and leads her behind the sofa.

MARIE

Raymond ... please ... I don't want to go with Monsieur Guy anymore. Oh!

RAYMOND has sex with her, unseen, on the floor behind the sofa

RAYMOND

There, that's better, isn't it? Best bit of prick you've had all night.

MARIE

Please don't let me go with Monsieur Guy anymore ...

RAYMOND

(*Breathless.*)

Let me finish, for God's sake! Ah! Ah! (*He comes.*)
Aaaah!

Pause. They get up. RAYMOND cuddles her.

RAYMOND

There. That was all right, wasn't it?

MARIE

Oh yes.

She returns to the sofa and sits down.

RAYMOND
What's the matter now? I look after you, don't I?

MARIE
Yes, Raymond.

RAYMOND
Well, then. (*Drinks his champagne.*)

MARIE
He'll kill me!

RAYMOND
Rubbish. Keep away from him. Arms' length.

MARIE
How can I? Please don't make me.

He looks down at her, and softens.

RAYMOND
Look, there's nothing to worry about. He's a gent. Aristocrat. He knows what he's doing.

MARIE
He's going to kill me.

RAYMOND
You'll have to take your chance.

MARIE
But you know he's dangerous.

RAYMOND
Shut up!

MARIE
He'll murder me, like he did Esmeralda!

RAYMOND

Shut your face this instant. I don't want to hear about it.

MARIE

He'll do it, I know. (*No response.*) You'll be a girl short!

RAYMOND

Plenty more where you came from. You'll have to take your chance. Try and keep his hands off your neck. Do what he wants. Get him through it. That's your job.

MARIE

A maid on their estate was found strangled as well.

RAYMOND

(*Twists her arm.*)

Another word, and you'll be living at a new address down the docks.

BERTHE enters.

RAYMOND

What are you doing? Get back to work!

BERTHE

They both want Francine.

BERTHE goes off to wash. MARIE weeps.

RAYMOND

And you can stop that. Stop it.

She sniffs, trying to stop.

RAYMOND

You got a good meal coming up.

MARIE

I'm not hungry. I'm ill, Raymond. I'm ill!

RAYMOND

Bollocks. Pull yourself together. I want you looking fresh tonight. You're the surprise.

MARIE

Oh no, please!

He finishes his drink and goes. BERTHE enters, and sits.

BERTHE

Ooh, you do look queer.

MARIE

I think I've come on again.

She goes behind the screen.

BERTHE
(Calls.)

All right?

MARIE
(From behind the screen.)

I don't know what to do. It won't stop.

BERTHE

Shove some cotton wool up. I hear the madman was in.

MARIE
(Off)

Yes.

BERTHE

No wonder.

MARIE comes out, and sits gingerly. She is deathly white.

BERTHE

Did he hurt you?

MARIE looks at her.

> **BERTHE**
> Tell you what, next time he comes – yell! Me and Francine'll be in there, scratch his eyes out. We don't care.

> **MARIE**
> Will you?

> **BERTHE**
> Yeah! Course!

She pours MARIE a glass of champagne, with a quick glance offstage.

> **BERTHE**
> Here...have some of this.

MARIE sips with difficulty.

> **BERTHE**
> Go on, knock it back! (*She is worried they will be caught.*) Listen, if you go sick, me and her will have to see to the lot of them. It's too much.

> **MARIE**
> I am trying.

She drinks. It seems as if she will faint. Her eyes roll up.

> **BERTHE**
> Oh Christ...

But she opens her eyes again, and clutches BERTHE in ecstasy.

> **MARIE**
> Berthe...Berthe! Believe! Please...please believe!

BERTHE

Oh, that's better. More like your old self again. (*She Gives MARIE more champagne.*) Put your feet up a minute. Get your strength back.

She lifts MARIE's feet onto the ottoman, even strokes the hair back off MARIE's face. MARIE catches BERTHE's hand, and clasps it to her.

MARIE

I must try to save you!

BERTHE

(*Disengaging herself.*)

Yes, okay.

FRANCINE crosses, and exits. MARIE mutters feverish prayers.

MARIE

Please, Berthe ... please ... Help me. Help me, sweet Jesus. (*Mutters prayers.*) Give me light ... (*Mutters.*) Mary, Mother of God ... (*Mutters to herself.*)

FRANCINE enters, flops, and closes her eyes. She awakens as MARIE, still muttering, falls off the ottoman onto her knees, still praying. She clasps her hands together and begins to move across the floor on her knees, with an incandescent look on her face.

FRANCINE

(*Sleepy.*)

Christ, what's up with her?

BERTHE

Ooh.

FRANCINE

What?

BERTHE

I give her some of that. (*Indicates champagne.*)

FRANCINE

Not on an empty stomach, you fool! Here...Marie...

But MARIE rises, in ecstasy, lifting her arms in intense, joyful prayer.

MARIE

Oh Lord... Thou who givest us light, and air, and all the beasts of the field, and of the forest. All the birds and those that swim in the deep and are unknown... Dearly beloved Lord, see this thy sister...blessed be the Lord who giveth me light... Oh! Lord, thou blesseth me beyond my knowing... Blessed be the name of the Lord!

She cries out in triumph, turns to the others, eyes staring.

MARIE

Blessed be the Lord who hath given Light where there was Darkness! Blessed be His Name! Love! In the name of Love!

She approaches, and attempts to clasp them.

MARIE

Now I can make you understand! Berthe... Love!

BERTHE

Eh?

MARIE

You understand Love... surely?

BERTHE

No.

FRANCINE

Yes, you do. (*To MARIE.*) She does.

MARIE

God Is Love!

FRANCINE

Sure.

MARIE

But not only love. (*She looks at them, waggish.*) Not only love. Oh no. No, no, no. Berthe!

BERTHE jumps.

BERTHE

What?

MARIE

Sister Therese was right! Why didn't I listen? It all makes sense!

This makes them jump again.

FRANCINE

Shut up. He'll hear you!

MARIE

Berthe, Berthe ... You like cooking, don't you?

BERTHE

She's gone mad.

MARIE

Cakes! If there's a cake, there has to be a cook! Am I right?

BERTHE nods.

MARIE

This chair – who made it?

BERTHE

Little Louie.

MARIE shakes her head.

BERTHE

No? I thought he did.

But MARIE shakes her head, smiling warmly.

FRANCINE

I know. God.

MARIE

Blessed be the name of the Lord. (*To BERTHE.*)
Berthe, you must see. Proof!

BERTHE groans.

MARIE

God. The Creator of all things. If there's no God, who made us? Where are we from? Why the world...the stars...the firmament?

BERTHE

Search me.

MARIE

Why the sun? Why the moon? Why air? Why light? Why anything? Someone must have created it. They must have. Otherwise we wouldn't be here. It wouldn't make sense. Things have to make sense!

FRANCINE
(*Sleepily.*)

Who says so?

MARIE

You can't believe everything's nonsense. You believe in evil...?

BERTHE

Oh yeah.

MARIE

Then you must believe in good. No, I know you. You believe in things making sense...and they do! Seeds sprout, plants grow, night follows day, the child becomes the man...

FRANCINE

(Mutters.)

We peg out.

MARIE

It's all around us, can't you see?

BERTHE

(Looking around.)

What?

MARIE

The affirmation! *(She touches things.)* We see... we hear... we feel! How can you not believe?

BERTHE

(Irritated.)

In what?

MARIE

In God... In Love! We're the children of Love! Love creates us and supports us. Love nourishes our spirit, keeps us alive. Believe, Berthe...use you dear sense, and believe! We're all the children of Love!

She floods.

                    MARIE

Ohh...

FRANCINE, instantly awake, jumps to her feet, and grabs a towel from the dressing table.

                  FRANCINE

Quick!

                    BERTHE

Christ!

                  FRANCINE

Here...

She hands BERTHE a piece of cloth from the mending basket. And gives another piece to MARIE.

                  FRANCINE

Quick, shove this up you before he comes. If you stain this ottoman, he'll kill us.

RAYMOND enters. They half-hide MARIE from his view.

                  RAYMOND

That's it for tonight, girls. No more casuals. You can get yourselves dolled up for the party. Marie's the surprise. Come and help me with the table.

FRANCINE throws a shawl over MARIE, and follows RAYMOND and FRANCINE off.

They return with a long table. RAYMOND is at one end, FRANCINE and BERTHE at the other. It is covered with a damask cloth, and has some food and dishes on it.

RAYMOND

(To MARIE.)

Come on, you. On your feet.

FRANCINE

She's feeling a bit faint. (*Whispers.*) You know, that Monsieur Guy, or whatever you call him.

He grunts.

FRANCINE

Leave her be. She'll be okay for later, know what I mean?

He nods and goes. FRANCINE and BERTHE follow him, soon returning with ornate silver dishes, and decorated food.

BERTHE

Ooh, lovely!

RAYMOND

Keep your thieving fingers off. (*Looks at his watch.*) Now make sharp and get dressed, all of you. We're late.

He goes. They cross to MARIE.

BERTHE

Marie?

FRANCINE

Marie? (*To BERTHE.*) I don't like the look of her.

BERTHE shoves FRANCINE aside, lifts MARIE, and shakes her. Then she drops her, and jumps back.

BERTHE

Ugh, it's blood!

FRANCINE

Where?

BERTHE

Coming out of her mouth. Ugh!

FRANCINE

Quick! Mop it up! Oh Christ. Marie ... Marie, love ...
Come on, love. Come on – wake up!

BERTHE

Marie, don't mess about. Come on!

FRANCINE

Shut up, he'll hear you! Marie ... Marie ...?

She leans over and straightens her up.

FRANCINE

It's no good. She's flat out.

BERTHE

What are we going to do?

She panics, grabs the champagne bottle, and sloshes it over MARIE's head.

FRANCINE

Mind out! You'll stain everything! Give it here.

She takes the bottle, and dabs champagne on MARIE's forehead. BERTHE gives her the glass and they try to make MARIE drink, without success.

BERTHE

Shall I get the old girl?

FRANCINE

No, she'll tell him.

They look down at MARIE.

BERTHE

Here – she's not dead, is she?

FRANCINE

Don't be so daft.

BERTHE lays her head on MARIE's breast.

BERTHE

I can't hear nothing.

FRANCINE

Let me have a go. (*She listens at MARIE's chest.*) I'm damned if I can.

BERTHE

And she's gone ever such a funny colour. All bluey-white.

FRANCINE looks at MARIE's face. Then she lifts her hand and feels for a pulse. She puts MARIE's hand down gently.

FRANCINE

Give us that glass.

BERTHE gives her a hand-mirror from the dressing table. FRANCINE puts it to MARIE's lips. She looks at the glass. BERTHE cranes in to see.

BERTHE

She is dead, you know.

BERTHE lets out a moaning screech.

FRANCINE

(*Hisses frantically.*)

Shut up!

BERTHE

What are we going to do?

FRANCINE

It's not our fault!

BERTHE

She said she felt ill. The sheets in her room are black with blood, you know. Smells terrible in there. Ugh! I feel funny.

FRANCINE

Sit down.

As BERTHE is about to sit on the ottoman . . .

FRANCINE

Not there!

BERTHE

Who's going to tell him?

FRANCINE

I'm not telling him.

BERTHE

Nothing to do with me.

FRANCINE

We could get changed.

BERTHE

Yeah. He might come in and find her.

FRANCINE

Then it's nothing to do with us.

BERTHE

We weren't here at the time.

FRANCINE

Right. She was fine when we left. Come on.

They go. Pause. RAYMOND looks in.

THE TREAT

RAYMOND

Look sharp, Marie. We haven't got all night. I'm going for the wine.

He leaves. Pause. FRANCINE enters, dressed as DEMETER, her breasts exposed, in pink, cream and yellow, with high gold boots. She totters across, and looks down at MARIE.

FRANCINE

Aw ... What a shame.

BERTHE enters. She's wearing very little and looks like a FAIRY at the top of the Christmas tree.

BERTHE

He's bringing the wine in, and they're coming. He says for Marie to get in the cake.

They look down at MARIE.

FRANCINE

Where's her dress?

BERTHE

Hanging up. (*Stares at FRANCINE, realising what she means.*) Oh, I couldn't! I couldn't touch her!

FRANCINE

I can't do it on my own. Here, catch hold of her. We can't leave her here. He'll know we've seen her! Come on!

BERTHE

Oh. All right.

The pick her up. FRANCINE taking her shoulders, BERTHE taking her legs.

BERTHE

Ooh, God, she's heavy. You wouldn't think it, would you?

FRANCINE

You've only got the legs.

BERTHE trips.

FRANCINE

What's the matter now?

BERTHE

Fell over her shoe.

She tries to fit it back on.

FRANCINE

Don't bother with that now. He'll be in here!

BERTHE

I can't do it. I can't!

FRANCINE

What's the matter with you?

BERTHE

I've never seen anybody dead before! I don't like it. I don't like dead people. I hate death!

FRANCINE
(Through her teeth.)
Will you come on!

They manhandle the body offstage. Pause. RAYMOND enters, and gives the table a quick inspection. VOICES off, as SIX MEN enter – including MONSIEUR HENRI, and GASTON, a restauranteur. TWO of the MEN are cuddling BERTHE, who giggles.

BERTHE

Ooh, stop it!

MAN #1 tickles her. She squeals.

MAN #1

She's a bit small, this one!

MAN #2

Bit of a tiddler, eh? We'll have to throw you back!

MAN #3
(Cuddling FRANCINE)

I've got a nice bit of flesh here!

HENRI

That's our lovely Francine. Didn't I say? Didn't I say?

MAN #1
(To BERTHE.)

Here's a pretty little rosebud mouth. Go all the way down, do you, darlin'?

BERTHE

Try me, and you'll find out, won't you?

MAN #4
(To GASTON)

I put it to him straight.

GASTON

Did you, by God?

MAN #4

I said to him: when did you last pay a dividend?

GASTON

By God! You didn't mince words then, did you?

MAN #4

I didn't! I say, they've got some real Parisian stuff here ...

RAYMOND
(Pushing through.)

Make way, gentlemen, make way for the guest of honour! Ladies and gentlemen, Mesdames et messieurs! Je vous présente ... His worship the Mayor!

The MAYOR enters – a large man, puffing a cigar. The others clap and bravo.

MAN #1

Bravo, bravo! The Mayor! I say! Bravo!

Another chorus of bravos.

MAYOR

Thank you! Thank you, my friends ...

RAYMOND

Silence for the Mayor, friends!

MAYOR

Thank you, thank you. Now, I'm not going to make a speech. You all get plenty of that.

A chorus of "No's."

MAYOR

I'd just like to offer a little vote of thanks to our friend Gaston, here, for the wonderful banquet we've just enjoyed at his restaurant. (*To RAYMOND.*) Seven courses, without the pudding. We'll have a job to do justice to your little spread – but we'll try.

Vociferous agreement.

MAYOR

We'll do our best. I see you've got trifle. Never trifle with trifle, eh? Ha ha ha!

They all laugh.

RAYMOND

One moment. One moment, Monsieur, if I may be so bold.

MAYOR

Eh, what? What's he up to?

RAYMOND

A little surprise, Monsieur le Mayor.

BERTHE

A surprise!

MAYOR

Not another dozen magnums of champagne? We've brought them with us, by the way. You can put your badger's piss away. Ha ha ha!

RAYMOND

Gentlemen, if we may have your attention. Francine – the lights, my dear, if you will. Berthe – la musique!

BERTHE puts on a gramophone record. RAYMOND swoops off.

The MEN laugh, waiting and chattering. RAYMOND returns, almost at once, wheeling on a huge 'CAKE,' with flaming candles on the top.

Laughter and applause.

MAYOR
(To GASTON)
Oh, not again. The second one tonight. And there'll

be another before the night's out. You think they'd
dream up something a bit different. No imagination.
No imagination. (*To RAYMOND.*) Bravo! Wonderful
surprise! Oh, and candles too!

               MEN

Blow them out! Blow out the candles! Come on,
Monsieur le Mayor! Lots of breath please! A good blow
now!

The MAYOR blows out the candles to much applause. RAYMOND
makes a theatrical gesture towards the cake.

               RAYMOND

Et voila!!

Nothing happens.

               RAYMOND

Voila!

Nothing happens.

               RAYMOND

Voila! Voila!

Laughter.

               MAYOR

What's the matter? Is she stuck?

Loud laughter. RAYMOND, furious, gives the cake a kick.

               RAYMOND

My apologies, Monsieur! Un moment, s'il vous plait.
Monsieur Raymond will take a look!

He waggles his behind saucily, lifts the lid of the cake, looks inside,
and bangs down the lid quick.

THE TREAT

MAN#2

Come on, come on ...

MAN #4

Yes, what have you got in there?

MAN #1

Pig is it? Couple of ducks?

MAN #3

(Cuddling FRANCINE.)

We've got those already!

HENRI

Come on, come on, come on! I know who it is. I know who it is! Surprise, surprise!

GASTON

Let's have a look!

RAYMOND

No! No! There's been a mistake. A little mistake ...

FRANCINE

(Coming forward.)

Gentlemen! Gentlemen! It's special! A surprise for the Mayor's eyes only!

RAYMOND

(Trying not to panic.)

Yes, yes!

FRANCINE

What's all this about champagne, M'sieur le Mayor?

RAYMOND

I'll open it at once.

MAYOR

No. You stay, Raymond. I want to see my gift. Tout le monde...into the salon. La Veuve awaits you.

BERTHE and FRANCINE herd the MEN out.

MAN #2

Surprise, eh?

MAN #4

If it's cake, we all want a slice, eh?

They go, laughing.

MAYOR

And now, my friend, let's see what we have here. Something gone wrong?

RAYMOND

No, no ... No, I assure you.

MAYOR

We'll see. We'll see ...

He approaches the cake.

MAYOR

I think I know how these things work. We've seen enough of them. Remember the little girl last year? Ah, ten years old. Now, that was a surprise. You'll have a lot to do to better that, my friend. Well, let's see.

He opens the cake – swinging it open sideways. Inside is MARIE, her face deathly white, dressed as the Virgin Mary, with lilies in her hands.

RAYMOND
(Whispers.)
Oh my God ...oh my God, oh my God ...

He crosses himself, terrified.

MAYOR
Well, well, well ... What have we here?

He puffs at his cigar, appraising the scene.

MAYOR
Well, well.

RAYMOND trembles.

MAYOR
You're a clever man, Raymond. You're cleverer than I gave you credit for. Bold too. I like that. I can use that in a man. *(Sharp.)* Who told you? How did you know?

RAYMOND
Told me? No-one. No-one, Monsieur le Mayor.

MAYOR
Hmmm. We'll talk about it later. No, you're a wag. You're a wag, sir. Last year, and now this! No, I like a man who takes the trouble to study me. Clear the stuff off that table. Just push it to one end.

RAYMOND
Sir?

MAYOR
Here, I'll give you a hand. There, that's enough space I think.

RAYOND makes to clear some of the puddings.

MAYOR

No, leave that. Give us a hand.

Petrified, RAYMOND helps him lay MARIE out on the table. The MAYOR pushes dishes aside, and then rests her head on a large salami.

MAYOR

(*As they move her.*)

No, quite imaginative. I like imagination. I knew you had an esoteric little business here. Still ... No, no, we must have a chat sometime. There. There, straighten her dress. Splendid. I congratulate you.

RAYMOND

Thank you, Monsieur.

MAYOR

Where did you get her from? The morgue?

RAYMOND

What!

MAYOR

Never mind. Discretion. But I shan't forget the favour. A real treat. Something I've wanted for a long time. Not easy to procure. I'm in your debt.

RAYMOND

Monsieur.

The MAYOR kisses him on both cheeks.

MAYOR

Now, if I may be allowed to enjoy my birthday gift? Before the others ...

RAYMOND

Of course.

He backs away. The MAYOR takes some pudding out of a bowl, and strokes it on to MARIE's hair.

> MAYOR
>
> *(To RAYMOND.)*

You don't object?

> RAYMOND
>
> Not at all. Not at all, Monsieur. Whatever your honour desires.
>
> MAYOR
>
> How peaceful she looks. Placid ... calm ... willing ... and silent. If only they were all like that. Oh, what a world we should have!

He scoops up some multi-coloured jelly, and rubs it in her face and hair.

> MAYOR
>
> There you are, my dear. You don't mind that, do you? You see? Not a murmur.

This is too much for RAYMOND. He wheels, and rushes off.

> MAYOR
>
> What a world! What a world!

He takes off his jacket, and hangs it up carefully. He puffs on his cigar, then puts it away with equal precision. He lets down his braces, undoes his fly buttons, and removes his trousers. He tries the table for solidness with his hands, then hoists himself on top of MARIE.

He throws away the lilies in her folded hands, and starts to fumble for her bosom and caress her.

> MAYOR
>
> Ah!

He continues to caress her, and rub food into her torso.

                    MAYOR

Ah! Ah! Ah! What a treat! What a treat! What a treat!

                                      Lights down.

The End.

Also from Quota Books . . .

PAM GEMS
Plays Two

Go West Young Woman
Nelson
Not Joan the Musical
King Ludwig of Bavaria

*

PAM GEMS
Plays Three

Betty's Wonderful Christmas
The Socialists
Guinevere
Ethel

MARS ATTACKS MEMOIRS
By Mila Pop

Reviews

A rare insight into the Tim Burton cult classic. Hear about Hollywood behind the scenes and the development of the Mars Attacks! movie. A must read for movie buffs and fans alike.

LUKE ETTENSPERGER

The Mini-Cooper of the literary world, this book is nippy and stylish, attentive to detail, with a disarming, quirky exterior that belies a deep intelligence and timeless design. Mila Pop is a great interviewer; her questions, as well as her delight at the responses Gems provides, show that she clearly loves the film. Jonathan Gems answers her questions generously and on many levels. He explains how the movie almost did not come about (the phrase 'madcap adventure' comes to mind) and offers funny and fascinating anecdotes about some of the people involved. He also gives us the inside skinny on how the film industry and Hollywood really work, and from there goes into how this paradigm can be seen throughout society. His great affection for Tim Burton and his girlfriend, Lisa-Marie, is very touching and transcends mere artistic collaboration. The book nails the sense of a collection of supremely talented people having a blast as they create unique and wonderful things – namely the movie itself, the friendships made along the way, and the interaction between Pop and Gems. It's an easy, happy read, over all too quickly. I look forward to more.

LEELA MILLER

A fantastic fun read. You will not be disappointed. It's like sitting on a couch with both Jonathan and Mila and hearing awesome stories on how a movie is written and put together.

PATRICK EVRARD.

I am so glad I bought this book 'cause I almost didn't after seeing the cover. Now I know the meaning of 'Never judge a book by its cover!' This is the book everyone needs to read. Our education and society would be so much better if this book was part of the school syllabus. It's very subversive and incredibly intelligent. Criticizes everything wrong with today's society and offers solutions. Unbelievable story, unbelievable writing. If I had to choose one book to read through eternity, this would be the one!

JOSH on AMAZON.CO.UK

Full of anecdotes about the film, its star-studded cast, the writer and director, and their struggles with the suited executives. Every page has a jewel to throw light upon the people behind the movies we love. Want to know what goes on behind the scenes in Hollywood? Here we see exactly what creatives go through to see their ideas brought to life by the mega-corporations. If you've ever seen Mars Attacks you will absolutely love this book.

WILLIAM HARWARD.

I found it fascinating that he and Tim Burton were able to take so many risks in this modern era of conglomerate films. His comments are a refreshing insight into a Hollywood which is in desperate need of being spruced up.

JUDE ZIETARA.

In Europe and South America, movies are called 'The Seventh Art.' In the USA, they are called 'The Industry.' After reading this insightful, funny, and sometimes shocking, book, I can see why.

MILANKO LUKOVIC.

A fascinating read about scriptwriting and filmmaking. I never knew how interesting the whole process was, and I enjoyed getting to know the stars and the crew. I was laughing all the way through.

COLIN PANRUCKER.

Mila Pop's lively and natural passion for people and their lives is infectious and fun. It will always leave you wanting more. The wacky Mars Attacks! is like nothing else, and so the wacky and hectic story of how it got made is fitting. The very touch-and-go nature of the movie industry is revealed. It can turn on a dime from gushing praise and promise to frozen over and aloof. Aspiring writers, directors, and actors take note! In Jonathan Gems, we see a man sustained by gratitude and the company of good people, self-possessed and of great calibre. Fully aware of others and soaking up the details of life. A true writer. He shows us that under all of the urgent and overblown dramatics and bravado of big movie-making are real people – flawed and brilliant. Generous with his many stories, you will likewise be left wanting more.

RO HACKETT

So very interesting getting new insights into the world of film and show business. What a clever man Jonathan Gems is too. So well read. I want to see the film again to pick up on all the extra things we now know.

DENNIS PIERCE.

This guy is amazing. He tries to tell you how we have no say or power when it comes to movies because of controlling rich people. Jonathan Gems you're my hero. Jonathan was trying to get out to the people that art is being held hostage.

TYLER on AMAZON.COM

WHO KILLED BRITISH CINEMA?
By Vinod Mahindru and Jonathan Gems

Reviews

Who killed British cinema? It's a good question – especially since us Brits used to have the second biggest film industry in the world and now it is practically non-existent. And the question gets explored with real vigour in this interesting and well put-together book.

It brings forth a mix of opinions whilst examining theories that could very well explain the 'death' of British cinema.

Not only is it refreshingly honest, but it is also very detailed, as it is richly supported by intriguing stats and thought-provoking quotes from credible individuals from the film industry (taken from pre-arranged interviews). Because of this, there is real insight within the copy and, as it has been thoroughly researched, you can find out more about the history of British cinema and its unfortunate decline in a succinct way. You don't have to pore over lengthy textbooks or wordy theories to grasp the timeline of events.

Overall, this makes for a riveting read that unpicks the political and cultural factors influencing media production and development over the decades and, if you are a film buff, you will particularly enjoy this in-depth piece of non-fiction. It even comes with a list of must-see British films!

HANNAH MONTGOMERY
www.whatson.guide

★★★★★ 5.0 out of 5 stars. **A Film Maker's Must Read!**

There is no shortage of resources for new and emerging filmmakers. There are courses, free and paid apps, some excellent and some not-so-good; there are many, many books written about every aspect of the art, from writing the script to where to stay in Cannes when you're sending your new baby out into a world of adoring soon-to-be fans. All of these, to a greater or lesser degree, have their uses but if, like me, you are involved in the production of shorts and /or features in the UK, there is one resource that will make you angry. Very angry. A book (and documentary film) that will make your blood boil and – if you're anything like me – wonder why you decided to become involved in the obviously pointless world of UK film making in the first place.

If it doesn't make you angry; if it doesn't make you want to scream in rage; if it doesn't make you say: "This has ALL got to change!" then you'd better go and do something else because, believe you me, you might think you love film and cinema, but you most certainly don't!

The book *Who Killed British Cinema?* by Vinod Mahindru and Jonathan Gems, is an in-depth and comprehensive look at the British film industry – or rather, the lack of it – from its glory days when it was the second largest in the world to the present day where there is not one single British movie studio, and 98% of the films in our cinemas are made by foreign entities.

Now don't get me wrong, I'm certainly not a xenophobic Brexiteer Little Englander who thinks everything 'foreign' is bad; far from it. I'm a Remainer who has spent many years of his creative life in Europe, who loves the cinema of Bergman, Fassbinder (Rainer Werner rather than Michael) and Truffaut, but who also grew up with – and has deeply rooted in his soul – the magnificent films of Michael Powell, Emeric Pressburger, Alberto Cavalcanti, Charles Crichton and David Lean – not to mention Terence Davies, Derek Jarman and Peter Greenaway. Films that truly express our national identity; what it means to be British with all its peculiar sensibilities. Films that show our individualities and uniqueness in a way that the current diet of pap served up at the multiplexes could never hope to achieve.

The book examines the way in which film funding has gone in this country. The role of such bodies as the BFI, BAFTA, the erstwhile

Regional Screen Agencies, Creative England and, most interestingly, the policy of successive governments that have led to the demise of our most successful creative industry.

Read it. Watch the documentary. Listen to what the ex-CEO's of these august bodies say about spending 65% of their agency's budget not on film production but on admin and salaries. Read about funding bodies that fund production companies owned by members of the funding bodies who granted the funds in the first place. Do this and don't get mad, I dare you!

This is not a negative book, nor a negative film. It is rather a call to arms for every filmmaker in the UK to say: "This is not right. This has to change."

I found it inspirational. I found that, though my blood boiled at the sheer injustice of it all, it has increased my determination to succeed ten-fold. As Buckminster Fuller is quoted at the end of the documentary film: "You never change things by fighting the existing reality. To change something, build a new model that makes the existing model obsolete."

If you buy one book about filmmaking, let it be this one. It will change your life and, who knows? maybe just help you to reinvent our beloved industry.

IAN MCLAUGHLIN MBKS

Q

website: www.quotabooks.com
email: info@quotabooks.com
Twitter: @Quotabooks

www.ingramcontent.com/pod-product-compliance
Lightning Source LLC
Chambersburg PA
CBHW070457120526
44590CB00013B/673